Up
from
the
Ghetto

Other Books by PHILLIP T. DROTNING

Black Heroes in Our Nation's History
A Guide to Negro History in America
A Job with a Future in the Petroleum Industry

Up
from
the
Ghetto

by Phillip T. Drotning
and Wesley W. South

COWLES BOOK COMPANY, INC.
NEW YORK

To Jayne and Mildred

Contents

Introduction

Although most history books give black men and women little credit for their achievements during 350 years in America, they have been "making it" since the day the first Africans were put ashore at Jamestown, Virginia, in 1619. Some blacks, indeed, achieved independent success as farmers and craftsmen even before slavery was given legal sanction by the courts.

Two of my previous books, *A Guide to Negro History in America*, published in 1968, and *Black Heroes in Our Nation's History*, published by Cowles Book Company in 1969, dealt with the long-neglected role of blacks in the growth and progress of the United States. Writing them proved to be a revealing as well as a rewarding experience.

Anyone, black or white, who undertakes black history as a new field of study is certain to be startled when he discovers the breadth and significance of the black contribution to America. History books do not ignore the collective contribution that millions of black slaves made to the development of the South, but they often underrate it. The individual contributions of countless other blacks—both slave and free—to our political, cultural, religious, social, and economic heritage have largely been overlooked, if not deliberately concealed.

Even more awesome than the breadth and magnitude of these contributions is the realization of the incredible odds against which they were achieved. One marvels at the stature achieved by a Benjamin Banneker, who triumphed over the indignity and repression of slavery by teaching himself reading, writing, and mathematics. Banneker wrote an almanac of such quality that it drew the praise of President Thomas Jefferson, and he developed such breadth of scientific and technical competence that he was selected to help Pierre L'Enfant lay out the grand design of Washington, D.C. This remarkable self-taught genius once constructed a clock after being given a fleeting glimpse of the inside of a watch!

Countless other blacks, slave and free, have demonstrated that no restraint imposed upon them, no ordeal demanded of them, no cruelty inflicted upon them, could break their spirit or quench their determination to achieve. One gains a new appreciation of the moral fiber of the nation's black population as he comprehends the trials that these fittest of the species have been required to endure.

During the colonial period and in the decades that preceded the Emancipation Proclamation, thousands of blacks exercised great ingenuity and courage to win their way out of bondage and achieve stature and affluence in a great variety of fields. Often, it is true, it was the assistance of a white benefactor that enabled them to gain the opportunity to do so. But, with or without such assistance, it took enormous determination, valor, and strength of character for them to triumph over a system that was coldly calculated to keep the black man "in his place."

As I studied the lives of blacks who had achieved success in another era and observed the qualities that had enabled them to triumph over seemingly insurmountable handicaps, I began to wonder whether any parallel could be drawn with the careers of blacks who are achieving stature in America today. Why does one black boy or girl find his way out of poverty and gain a respected place among his white peers while another never rises above the deprived circumstances in which he was born?

One day, reading Richard Bardolph's superb study of early black leaders, *The Negro Vanguard*, I came across the words of an unidentified but "brilliant, famous, and prosperous Negro."

"Every successful Negro can be accounted for by family, by the people he gets to know, and any of hundreds of other variables. It's all a matter of people having a chance. There is no equality of opportunity for anybody, white or Negro, anywhere. Lots of people with immense potentials never get anywhere simply because they don't have the chance—the right parents, the right geographical and educational opportunities, accidental deliverance from the temptations that can ruin a man's chances in ten minutes. The people who don't have these breaks don't have any choice in the matter, and neither do those who do."

The quotation troubled me because, although it certainly contained an element of truth, it seemed an oversimplification that ignored those elements of human character that are a vital factor in individual success or failure. Certainly it is not only opportunity, but the wit to recognize it and the courage and determination to exploit it that must be involved in the success of one deprived black child and the failure of another.

Wesley South and I wrote this book hoping to discover whether there are consistent elements of human behavior that enable some to succeed while others fail. We selected, at random, without any detailed knowledge of their early years, fourteen black men and women who have won contemporary recognition for achievement in a variety of fields. At the outset, we anticipated that among them would be some who owed their success to the fact that daddy owned the store. Instead, to our astonishment, they all proved to be the product of impoverished ghetto environments, and many of uneducated if not illiterate parents. While chance was an element in the success of some, sheer guts, determination, and an unquenchable desire to succeed emerged as the more significant keys to their achievement.

Except for casual references to the deprivation they knew in their youth, most of what has been written so far about distinguished contemporary blacks deals with the period after they achieved success. In his interviews with the subjects of this book, Wesley South, a black man himself, probed their early years and drew from them candid recollections of the backgrounds from which they struggled to achieve the stature they enjoy today.

For the most part, the early childhood of the personalities described here was not significantly different from that of millions of youngsters who live in poverty in the nation's villages and cities today. We hope that the experiences of these successful black Americans will provide hope and encouragement to young people who are similarly deprived and do not yet see in the nation's growing opportunities the brighter future that can be theirs.

We also hope that adult readers, black and white, will find in the wisdom and example of these black men and women their own opportunities to help restore our divided society and insure that every child born in this country will have a chance to share fully in the dream that is America.

Phillip T. Drotning
Glenview, Illinois
September 15, 1969

Up
from
the
Ghetto

1

Ernie Banks

Mr. Cub

When Ernie Banks walked through the Texas heat to the commencement platform at Booker T. Washington High School in Dallas in 1950, he was proud, though uncomfortable, in his first "store-bought" suit. His mother had discovered it, after much desperate searching, in the Goodwill Industries store. It had cost her twenty cents.

Finding a garment worthy of the occasion at a price her meager purse could manage was a satisfying triumph for Essie Banks. She and Eddie, the boy's father, wanted their first-born son to be properly dressed for so auspicious an occasion, but the Banks family income left little margin for clothing. Other needs take priority when you are black, broke, and have thirteen hungry children in the house. Hand-me-downs are grudgingly accepted, of course, by the younger children in most large families, but even the oldest of the Banks boys had lived all his nineteen years in clothing discarded by somebody else.

Ernie still recalls that day vividly, mostly because only three of the thirteen Banks children had the tenacity, desire, or good fortune to finish high school. But he also remembers it because of the pleasure he took in wearing his first new suit.

"When I got over there to graduation the fellows were all

1

surprised because they had never seen me in anything dressed up," Ernie recalls. "I always wore jeans or something like that. This was a dark suit, not very well tailored, but it fit me well enough and I sure felt good."

Ernie doesn't talk much about those dismal days in Dallas. As the undisputed champion among eternal optimists, his conversation is more apt to be studded with aphorisms describing the rosy future that awaits his cherished Chicago Cubs. It is only among intimates that he will shyly confess that the graduation suit still hangs in his closet, crowded by the fancier threads that he has acquired during his years as one of the most durable stars in the National Baseball League.

And why not? The suit certainly is an appropriate symbol of Ernie's transition from the bleak poverty of Dallas's black ghetto to fame and fortune in the second largest city in the United States. No one who saw Ernie at his graduation, nervous and perspiring in his Goodwill suit, foresaw the day when a hard-bitten white sportswriter would call the black athlete "an advertisement for the whole human race."

That Ernie Banks could achieve the respect, admiration, and, indeed, the affection of millions in Chicago and elsewhere stems from a remarkable combination of gentleness, good humor, determination, and guts. His thirty-eight years —even the best ones—have found him constantly among the have-nots of society, first in the slums of southwest Dallas, and later with his hapless baseball team in the "cellar" of the National League, often as the only jewel in the tarnished diadem of the Chicago Cubs.

After seventeen years in the majors, the lithe black athlete, still weighing in at a trim 180 pounds, and with the grace of a tiger in his six-foot-one-inch frame, continues to give his fans more than they have any right to expect. To be sure, he is not the ballplayer he was a dozen years ago, but he has, after all, been a candidate for retirement for at least five years. In fact, for a brief period after Leo Durocher took over as manager of the Cubs, Ernie actually was retired to the role of player-coach.

There is little doubt that Durocher wanted to retire him totally, but even that irascible and uncompromising tyrant knows his own limitations. He doubted, if he fired Ernie, that he could survive the wrath of the first baseman's devoted fans, so he thought he would ease him out gracefully. Durocher must now congratulate himself daily on that bit of unaccustomed forbearance, for on opening day Ernie was in the starting lineup at first base. Three seasons later, with the Cubs in first place, he was still fielding hot grounders like a kid and slamming the baseball out of the park.

Some Chicagoans see him as the friendly guy who is always willing to sign a flock of autographs when some kid spots him getting off an airplane at O'Hare field. Others smile with approval when Ernie speaks at a banquet in behalf of some of the inner city's underprivileged youngsters, or trots off to a hospital between games to deliver an autographed baseball to a bedridden fan.

To a vast television audience, he is a sports oracle on Channel 9, greeting his viewers from "the bee-yoo-ti-ful confines of Wrigley Field, where the sun always shines." His spirit is literally unquenchable for he sees sunshine even on days when the only fans to reach the park are the ones who know how to swim.

At other times Ernie is a successful businessman: a partner in the first Ford automobile franchise ever awarded to blacks, or an executive out winning new accounts for the integrated Seaway National Bank. Add to that his work as a member of the Chicago Transit Authority, or on the Board of Managers of the Chicago Metropolitan YMCA, and you have the portrait of a leading citizen whose achievements are difficult to reconcile with the handicaps of his heritage and the environment in which he spent his youth.

Ernie Banks was born in Dallas on January 31, 1931, in the depths of the worst depression the nation has ever seen.

His father, no longer a youngster, had returned to his native community of Marshall, Texas, after serving in the United States Army. There, at thirty-eight, he met and married a young girl from the nearby village of Shreveport, Texas. Essie Banks was only sixteen on their wedding day.

Eddie Banks and his young bride soon moved to Dallas and settled down in a cramped and flimsy house that huddled on the edge of an unpaved lane called Katy Street. Ernie's father worked around Dallas when and where he could, long hours for short pay, picking cotton, sweating as a common laborer on construction jobs, or wielding a broom or mop when more rewarding employment was not available. Ultimately, when times improved, he landed a reasonably secure but ill-paid job in a grocery store. It provided barely enough to feed and house the steadily expanding family.

"Dad loved baseball," Ernie recalls. "He played semi-pro ball with a team around Marshall and later with a local Dallas team, but he was a man who worked hard all his life, from sunup to sundown, keeping a large family together. He'd leave early in the morning and we'd seldom see him until after dark. He spent a little time with us on weekends, playing catch mostly, and wanted us boys to be baseball players. Of course, there were no real opportunities in those days—in the early forties—until Jackie Robinson came into baseball. That was when my father first started thinking about one of us making the major leagues, but it was just a dream. I don't think any of us really believed it was possible. Jackie was just a hopeful exception and we couldn't visualize a time when there would be more than 150 blacks in major league baseball, as there are today.

"We lived in a wooden frame house—what you called a shotgun house, straight through from front to rear. I can remember that we always put paper on the outside for the Christmas holidays, to keep out the cold. Our only heat was from an old round-bellied wood stove. The bathroom? It was just where you would expect—out back.

"I guess you would have to say that the house wasn't very much. It was small, and when I think about it I wonder how we managed with fifteen of us in it. All I remember is that after my brothers were born—until I left home—I always slept three in a bed.

"The yard was small, too, and that posed some problems for a bunch of lively kids. The neighbors didn't like us playing in their yard, and I guess I can't blame them because we were always putting a baseball through one of their windows. My uncle finally moved in next door to us so we could have more room to play in. He didn't have any children, so we fenced in both yards, and things were better after that."

Until he reached his teens that house and yard and the ghetto that surrounded them formed the boundaries of Ernie's existence.

"There were about twenty-five kids in the same block all about the same age, and except for school and church our whole world was there. We were close to the Borden plant and the icehouse, which meant a great deal to us because we could sometimes get the overflow of ice cream or a piece of ice for summer refreshment."

As Ernie grew older he managed to find work to supplement the meager earnings of his father and provide a few extra necessities for the growing brood of children. He sold newspapers, picked cotton, and worked in a hotel as assistant to the janitor. Some weeks he made as much as twenty dollars, but he didn't go to the movies or spend it on himself. The money went to his mother to help feed the family and pay the rent. Ernie spent his spare time at sports or hanging around the YMCA. He always wanted to join the "Y," but, with the family circumstances as they were, he couldn't afford to be a member. Remembering that, he now spends a great deal of time raising funds to support the Chicago YMCA's inner-city projects.

Ernie doesn't recall being any hungrier than the other children in his neighborhood, but he acknowledges that the food they had was very plain and there was never much of it.

"Dinner was our critical meal and Sunday was the big day," Ernie remembers. "Sundays we had chicken or something like that, corn bread, hoe cakes, beans and rice and chick peas, neck bones, and probably some kind of greens. We were always kind of light on breakfast; usually we had oatmeal. It was cheap and it filled you up. A lot of people are still eating like that. It was about the cheapest way of getting by in the morning if you didn't put milk on it—especially for a large family. We never did have much milk, I guess, because during the Depression we were living on food rations—mostly staples like flour that came on the welfare truck. My father always worked when he could, but the family was on relief in the early thirties because there just wasn't any work."

Ernie's recollections of his Dallas childhood reveal no tinge of bitterness or regret. He and his five brothers and seven sisters shared the poverty of their Dallas ghetto not really aware that they were deprived because it was the only living standard they had ever known. If they were poor so were their neighbors, and they were spared the embittering contrasts that trouble so many young people today.

"I just thought that was the way things were," Ernie says. "We never had anything, and being brought up the way we were I never had a burning desire to have more than we had. Actually, when I look back, they were happy times. My father never showed signs that we were down and out. He had a happy attitude and assured us that somehow we would always have what we needed. As a result, I never had the feeling that we were really poor."

Despite his father's interest in baseball, Ernie didn't get

really involved in organized sports during his years in the neighborhood elementary school. He did play softball with a team at St. Paul's Methodist Church, which his family attended faithfully every Sunday, and also played on YMCA teams. When he entered junior high school he began to play softball and volleyball but didn't take either very seriously.

His lack of involvement in the earlier years may have stemmed from his innate shyness. In contrast to the outgoing baseball star of today, the youthful Ernie was quiet, almost withdrawn except with his family and close friends, and extremely bashful in the presence of girls. He still remembers the kidding he suffered when he took his first girl to a dance and she deserted him to go home with somebody else.

"Sports were always a kind of a sideline in my life," Ernie recalls. "It wasn't until I got to high school that I got serious about them. A friend of the family encouraged me to go out for football and talked the coach into giving me a chance. He put me at end, and it developed me. It was a good part of my life because I began to associate with other fellows who didn't come from my community."

Those new associations helped Ernie overcome his reticence and gain confidence in himself. Even in high school he began to reveal the spirit, determination, and natural grace and timing that are the hallmarks of a great athlete. Although, by his own admission, he "wasn't the brightest student," he enjoyed school, stayed out of the troubles that befell many of his friends, and credits much of his success to the encouragement he received in school and from his parents.

"I had one high school coach who motivated me a great deal," Banks recalls. "He always told us that we had to fight for things, that we couldn't expect from life any more than we were willing to put in it ourselves. I always remembered that, and, although getting into the major leagues was mostly a matter of luck, when that lucky moment came I was prepared for it. A fellow happened to come along and see me play in high school and I guess he liked what he saw because he said, 'How would you like to play semi-pro ball?' I was so surprised that I said I didn't know; I'd have to talk to my mother first. I did talk to her and wound up in Amarillo with the Colts when I was only seventeen years old.

"I gave them everything I had and really enjoyed it. Then one day this guy said, 'I'm going to recommend you for the Kansas City Monarchs.' So I went to Kansas City and when I arrived they said you're going to play shortstop and bat seventh, and I played that day and got four for seven.

"Then came September 7, 1953, and I was sitting in a hotel room in Chicago, the season just about over, talking with Bill Dickey, one of my teammates who came from Shreveport, Louisiana. There was a long winter ahead, and we were both wondering what we were going to do next. The phone rang, and it was our manager, who said he wanted Bill and me to meet him in the lobby at seven o'clock the next morning.

"We didn't know what he wanted but we were there promptly, and the three of us got into a cab. We were riding along, just talking, and didn't even think to ask where we were going. All of a sudden the cab pulled up at Wrigley Field, and we went into the office and met the manager of the Cubs. Without any preliminaries he said, 'You guys look pretty good, and we're going to sign you with the Cubs.'

"We were both stunned, and before we recovered enough to say anything he went right on talking.

" 'Dickey,' he said, 'we think you can pitch, and we're going to sign you to a contract at Cedar Rapids, Iowa. We're going to let you go home now and you can join the team out there next season.'

"Dickey was thrilled to death.

"Then he turned to me and said, 'Ernie, we think you can play here right now. The club is on the road, but be back here on the eighteenth, and we're going to sign you to a major league contract right now.'

"OOOOOOO-EEEEEEE! I was thrilled to death.

"I called home and told them I was going to play in the major leagues. Then I left Chicago and played the last game with the Monarchs in Pittsburgh, and they bought me a ticket and sent me back to Chicago. I checked in at the Sheraton-Lincoln and soon got a call saying that they would pick me up in the morning. I went out the next day and worked out, and I remember how excited I was when I watched the Cubs play a home series with the Dodgers. I had played exhibition ball with Jackie Robinson and Roy Campanella and still remembered some encouraging words I got from Jackie. He said, 'Hey, you can really hit that outside pitch. That's what you got to hit to get in the major leagues.'"

Ernie's first appearance with the Cubs was something less than spectacular. Curt Simmons was pitching and Ernie went nothing for three and made one error. The Cubs lost, 16–3. But Ernie played in ten of the few remaining games, pounded out two home runs, and finished the 1953 season with a batting average of .314.

The Cubs knew that they had a ballplayer.

In 1954, his first full year with the Cubs, Ernie turned in a .275 batting average, hit nineteen homers, and batted in seventy-nine runs. It was a respectable season, but it was in 1955 that the agile shortstop really began to flourish. By the time the season ended he had shattered two major league records. His forty-four home runs were more than any major league shortstop had ever hit in a season. Among them were five grand-slam homers, also a new record for the major leagues. He still holds that record and broke his own home run record in 1958.

That same 1958 season and the two that followed marked

9

the peak of Ernie's career. In 1958 he won his first National League Most Valuable Player award, and he captured it again in 1959, becoming the only National League player to win it two years in a row. In 1958 he led the league with 47 home runs and 129 runs batted in, ending the season with a batting average of .313. The following year he settled for 45 home runs, but again led the league with 143 runs batted in. And, perhaps just to prove that he was more than a hitter, he set a new major league record for fielding percentage by a shortstop—a near perfect .985.

In 1960, although he made the difficult switch from shortstop to first base, Ernie kept up the pace. He again led the league with forty-one home runs. Meanwhile, he played six full seasons without missing a game, which is still a record in the National League.

During most of his career with the Cubs Ernie has been the one bright spot in an otherwise dismal organization. Fans who wanted to check the Cubs' league standing had learned to save time by reading the table from the bottom up. In 1966, with the Cubs once again in the cellar, Leo Durocher was summoned to rescue the club from two decades of oblivion. Leo, with customary tenderness, announced that he would clean house on the ball club if he had to "back up a truck."

Durocher must have considered his aging first baseman as a prime candidate for space on the truck. Ernie had passed thirty-five and during the 1963 season his performance had been far short of the spectacular earlier years. His health was bad and he missed thirty-two games, hit only eighteen homers, and his batting average dropped to .227. He improved in the 1964 and 1965 seasons, but in 1966 he was not the ballplayer of old, not even the hitter he had been in his freshman year with the Cubs.

Durocher, however, dared not risk the summary dismissal of the only Cub who had sustained the feeble hopes of Wrigley Field fans during all those lean years. Thus it was that he compromised by naming Banks a "player-coach," which fooled none of the pallbearers who were now convinced that "Old Ern" had had it, at last. Happily, however, Durocher didn't convince Banks.

Although the outspoken Chicago Cubs' manager and his star first baseman are temperamental opposites, they proved to be good for each other. Ernie worked hard in spring-training camp. His health had improved and so had his hitting, and Durocher had him in the lineup on opening day.

The black first baseman holds no ill will toward his manager because of Durocher's low initial regard for his worth. On the contrary, Ernie credits the salty Irishman with contributing greatly to his continuing success and has often said that he regrets not having had Durocher as his manager earlier in his career.

"Leo makes me work harder to get that little extra that you need for success," Banks says. "I wish there had been someone like him around early in my career. You might resent his efforts at first, but all of a sudden you realize that he has turned you into a better ballplayer—not only a better ballplayer but a better man. He's made me go for that little extra that you need to win."

One suspects that these humbly grateful comments give Durocher more credit than he deserves, for there is no evidence in Ernie's career or his attitude to suggest the need for motivation outside himself. Throughout his career Banks has never ceased striving to improve his performance, to do a little better than his best.

Throughout most of his career Banks has always scoffed at suggestions that he might someday become a manager. Lately, however, one senses that his constant need for new challenges is causing him to have second thoughts about that. In one interview in 1969 he confessed that he would like to be a major league manager, and the first black man to make it, but is uncertain whether his personality is suited to the role.

"Could I push other people, make them give that little extra?" Banks asked. "I think I could. In the beginning I thought differently, but since I've been around Durocher I think I can push a player, get that little extra from him.

"I kind of marvel at people who have this knack of leading," he added. "The young guys on this team respect Mr. Durocher. They do what he wants them to do because they know they are going to benefit from it. I like that. It thrills me to see it because we are living in a time when many people don't respect authority. They need the example of men like Durocher and Lombardi, who demand obedience and respect and teamwork, and then prove that everybody profits from it."

There is little doubt that many Americans, particularly black youngsters, envy Banks for his baseball career, the glamour and acclaim that go with it, to say nothing of a salary that once reached sixty-five thousand dollars a year. Actually, Ernie is not playing baseball because he considers it the ideal career for him. Like many other black youngsters who were born in a time when sports and entertainment were the only profitable fields open to them, Ernie chose baseball because he was good at it and it was something that white society would let him do.

Ernie really wanted to be a lawyer, and he still speaks nostalgically of the reasons why a law career appealed to him.

"Law is a good field," he says. "It's helping people when they are in trouble, and I've always had this feeling that I like to help people. Law gives you a real chance because our people don't normally think of the legal aspects of things. They get into trouble buying things on time and in many other ways because they don't understand what the law can do to them. If I had been a lawyer I could have shown our people what's right and what's wrong, and kept others from taking advantage of them."

The current generation of black youngsters, Ernie believes, has much broader opportunities open to it. He points to the many businesses and industries that are actively recruiting black employees, and even providing training programs to qualify them for employment.

He believes that black people must be militant in seeking enlarged opportunities and true freedom for their race, but he has little sympathy for militance that lacks real purpose.

"There are certain things that you have to fight for, not by looting or burning, but by letting society know that you will demand your rights and will use every legal means to get them.

"I'm glad to see the emphasis on black pride and black power. Black people must find pride in themselves and in their heritage. But I don't agree with the guys that say in order to find pride in your blackness you have to hate everything that is white. That's just plain wrong. We shouldn't hate anybody. Black people have to get along in the world, not just among themselves. If you want to get a good job, or get into business, you've got to live with other people including the white ones.

"I think that the black leaders, the black businessmen and people in professional life, black athletes, all of us who are black and have made it should take a little more stock of ourselves and see what we can do to help black youngsters who have admiration for us and have found us kind of distant. We've got to give them a hand—a goal. But we've got to have help from the white man. It is a mistake to believe that we can do it all by ourselves any more than the Irish or the Italians escaped from the ghetto without help from people outside their community."

Banks feels that white America is becoming more realistic about the relationship between racism and discrimination and the problems that face the nation, and more understanding of the historic difficulties that have faced black people in their efforts to make a place for themselves in the mainstream of American life. With that understanding, more white people are trying to help improve conditions in our society, and business is becoming more deeply involved. Government and business together, he says, are going to make opportunities available to those black people who are willing to prepare themselves to take advantage of them.

Although his own performance in high school was not outstanding, Ernie places a high premium on education and training for skills as the means through which black Americans can win a position of equality in American life. Despite the status and financial security he has already won for his own family, he is still adding to his own education. Ernie has taken a number of extension courses at the University of Chicago and even during the baseball season last year he found time for a correspondence course in banking.

The baseball star's greatest concern is for young people—among them his own nine-year-old twin sons and six-year-old daughter. He sees in them the hope for a brighter future for people of all races. His eyes light up when he talks of what he wants for his children and his words contain seeds of wisdom that are worth remembering for any young person who wants to make the most of his life.

"Most of all," says Ernie, "I want my children to have the best education that I can afford. I want them to be independent rather than dependent. I want them to stand on their own feet. I want them to be leaders rather than followers, to get out and do something good on their own, rather than just following the crowd.

"I see so many people, so many young kids, who just follow the crowd. They don't really know what they want to do so they let others decide their course for them. Young people have to learn to make their own decisions, to make up their own minds, to decide what they want to be and stick to it."

Ernie deplores the tendency of so many city youngsters to join street gangs that have no purpose. He believes that they lead kids into activities that they would avoid if they were thinking for themselves rather than following the crowd.

"Don't depend upon someone else to make your decisions for you," he warns his youthful audiences. "Think for yourself and do what is right for yourself. If you just go along with the crowd it may be the wrong crowd and you'll find yourself tangled up all the time. You have to decide yourself when it's time to quit, time to get off the street, time to go home. That's important in living. Too many people don't know how to discipline themselves. They don't know when to say 'I've had enough and I'm going home,' or 'I'm driving too fast and I'm going to slow down.' "

It depresses Ernie when he sees kids who write dirty words on buildings, curse on the streets, engage in petty thievery, or get hooked on dope.

"I suppose that it makes them feel big when they do those things that show no respect for others or for authority, but it saddens me because I know they're not going to feel very big when they have ruined their lives because of it.

"I remember when I was seventeen I had a good friend —we went to Amarillo together—who got involved with marijuana. I could have smoked pot, too, but I didn't. After we got back to Dallas he got nabbed and spent a couple of years in the state penitentiary. I've thought about that a lot. We played ball together, roomed together, and I went to the Cubs while he went to jail. All because he got involved with the wrong people and I was lucky enough not to.

"When I went to the Cubs there were only a handful of blacks in the major leagues. Today there are more than 150. Nobody cares anymore what color you are. All they care is whether you're good. That isn't true just in sports; it's true in every walk of life.

"If I were a teen-ager today I'd set a goal for myself. I wouldn't worry about how poor I was, or how black I was, or how alone I was. I'd decide what I wanted to be—a lawyer, or doctor, or businessman—and then I'd go do what I had to do to be it.

"I wouldn't be afraid to ask for help. I'd go to people and agencies and schools and businesses and ask, 'What can you do to help me to be better, to get a good job, to have a better life than my parents had, a better life than I'm living now?'

"I know that many kids can't get that kind of help from their parents, but that isn't the end of the world. The way things are today they can get it someplace.

"Another thing, when I talk to school kids I tell them they've got to learn to stick with it. Our schools may not be the best, and what they are learning may not always seem relevant to getting a job, but any education is better than no education at all. You can't get a really good job without it.

"I tell them to stop making excuses for themselves because they are black, but instead to be proud of their blackness. If they are they'll know they can make it, that they can be better than the guys who try to put them down."

Throughout his life Ernie has proved that he could be better than a lot of other guys, but he has never let his success go to his head.

"I found out long ago that it is important to be nice to other people. I also discovered that it is important to be part of a team. If you ever let your success convince you that you are better than your team or your organization, then you are unable to become part of either one. If you think that way then you are really all alone."

Even at the age of thirty-eight, Ernie faced the 1969 season with the enthusiasm and determination of a rookie just embarking on a career in the major leagues. Although he had a new two-year contract in his pocket, he knew that this season might offer his last chance at a long-cherished goal—the opportunity to play in baseball's crowning event, the World Series.

Banks did not covet the Series for glory. To him it was simply another chance to prove himself—not to the world, but to Ernie Banks. Describing his feelings as he relaxed in the hot spring sun at the Cubs' Arizona training camp, Ernie said:

"This is my biggest opportunity in baseball. If I failed to do the things this year that I really want to do to help the Cubs win the Eastern Division title and then the championship, I would be a most unhappy person.

"When you're not on pennant-winning clubs you always have this feeling: 'I don't know whether I'm a clutch player or not.' I've never been challenged to make the big hit or the big play with a title at stake. That kind of competition and challenge has never been there in my career. I want to see how it feels."

After Ernie's many years of stellar competition there are few Cubs fans who share his doubts about his capacity under fire. They have seen him salvage too many ball games in tight situations. But Ernie isn't content with the acclaim of his fans. He has to be satisfied with himself. That's why the World Series test is so important to him. As he puts it:

"Even if I didn't play baseball anymore in my life, I would always remember this: 'Gee, I don't know how good I would have been under pressure—real pressure, that is.'"

The 1969 season opened with Ernie as confident as ever, and apparently his enthusiasm was contagious, for the Cubs leaped into first place with their opening game. By early September they were out in front of the National League's Eastern Division by nine full games.

The fans at Wrigley Field were ready to stand in line for World Series tickets when the New York Mets suddenly caught fire, and the Cubs' lead evaporated in an eight-game losing streak. From then until the end of the season the

Cubs could do nothing right, and the Mets could do nothing wrong. When the season ended, the Mets had the Eastern Division title, and the Cubs were eight games out, in second place.

In any other season a second-place finish would have had Cubs fans tearing up the seats in unrestrained joy, but in 1969 they had tasted total victory for much too long. Chicago was bitterly disappointed by the outcome, and so was Ernie Banks. Once again he had missed his long-sought ambition to test himself in a World Series game.

But as usual, losing the title didn't turn Ernie off. It was just another adversity which he met without despair, accepting it as a springboard from which to leap to greater heights in the future.

Optimist that he had always been in the worst of circumstances, Ernie could scarcely be expected to give up on a club that finished in second place. Besides, he still had a year to go on his contract, and another series was coming up next year.

Why worry? He wasn't even forty yet!

2

Jesse Jackson

The Now *Look in Religion*

Jesse Jackson was a boy of only nine or ten, living in an unpainted cottage in the ghetto of Greenville, South Carolina, when he first experienced the exhilaration that comes to those who can command the attention of an audience.

The year was about 1950—he isn't quite sure—and the occasion was the delivery of the first television set to the impoverished black neighborhood in which he and his family lived.

"I remember that day very well," the Reverend Mr. Jackson says today. "That television set was a real luxury in our community. The owner's house was like a movie theater, with people crowding in to see 'The Lone Ranger' on TV.

"I got involved because in those days they didn't have any Huntley-Brinkley. The television news used to come across the set so you had to read. There'd be almost sixty people jammed in the corners and out in the yard peeking at the television, but in that whole crowd I was the only one who could read the words coming across the screen!

"I remember that at the time it made me feel kind of big. It wasn't until I got a little older that I realized how pitiful that really was—all of those adults there and none of them could keep up with the news."

That episode was but one of many vivid childhood

recollections that ultimately fired young Jesse's determination to become an activist in the civil rights movement and attempt to unite his race in the struggle for political, social, and economic power. It also taught him the critical importance of education as the basis for individual and collective black progress. Today he is one of the leading apostles of the nonviolent militance espoused by his tutor and idol, the late Dr. Martin Luther King, Jr.

Although still a young man—he is only twenty-eight—Reverend Jackson is a brilliant strategist, a persuasive and inspiring orator, and an imposing figure wherever he appears. A superb athlete since high school days, his muscular 215 pounds are solidly distributed over his six-foot-two-inch frame. The piercing eyes in his handsome face are almost hypnotic in their magnetism.

Perhaps more than any other black leader in America, Reverend Jackson has charisma, that indefinable quality of personality that inspires his followers and fires them with courage and determination they didn't know they had. Nowhere is this more apparent than at his Saturday morning meetings, when as many as five thousand of his followers overflow the Capitol Theater, at 79th and Halsted Streets, on Chicago's south side, which serves as Jackson's church. Young and old, rich and poor, black and white, they are entranced by the Operation Breadbasket choir, which belts out old-time spirituals with a boogaloo beat, molding the listeners into a seething, swaying mass of emotional humanity. Thus aroused, they are fired with zeal and determination by the power of their leader's voice and the magic of his words.

Mr. Jackson is a clergyman, but more conventional clerics would be as appalled by his style as he is by their irrelevance. Almost flamboyant in dress and manner, he is apt to appear in his pulpit wearing a dashiki, or bell-bottom trousers and a black turtleneck shirt. He can identify with any audience, altering his mood and manner and sometimes his speech to suit the occasion. He can be austere, even haughty, and speak with almost scholarly precision when he delivers an ultimatum to a white business group, but he lapses easily and naturally into a corn-pone dialect when enlisting new followers among the young blacks in the ghetto streets.

Unlike the black ministers who for generations have used religion as an opiate to dull the pain and ease the misery of their congregations, Reverend Jackson is a powerful evangelist who commands his flock to seek their promised land in the present, not wait submissively to find it in the hereafter. His vehicle is Operation Breadbasket, the economic program of the Southern Christian Leadership Conference. As its director, he has caused the heads of some of the nation's largest corporations to tremble in their walnut-paneled suites. More important, he has induced them to open their doors to black employees, provide training programs to qualify blacks for more rewarding jobs, and patronize black suppliers of goods and services.

The fiery preacher sees himself as a catalyst of black economic power, which he views as the most potent weapon in the struggle of blacks to obtain a fair share of the nation's affluence. He deplores purposeless violence as a means of achieving black goals, asserting that "a man is not made up of muscles and a quick trigger finger; a man is one who has an enlightened mind and a compassionate heart."

"I'm a preacher," Mr. Jackson says, "but primarily I'm an organizer and a programmer. In a sense the civil rights movement is a drama, but you have to keep setting the stage and creating scenes that people can act their way out of if they are to make maximum progress. When I preach I try to energize the people to keep in the fight and not give up.

"We are trying to develop the kinds of programs that will generate power for black people to make decisions about the things that are relevant to their lives. It is when people are involved en masse that they are at their maximum political power. Part of what we do is keep people awake. The greatest challenge in the civil rights movement is to wake people up, because most people are so full of fear that they lie to themselves and lull themselves to sleep."

Reverend Jackson misses few chances to demonstrate that he holds no awe of the white power structure and is ready and willing to fight. One such opportunity came the day after Dr. King's assassination, at a meeting of the Chicago City Council. Mayor Richard Daley, who had been an implacable and outspoken foe and critic of Dr. King, read a eulogy to the slain preacher that began, "The life of Dr. King and his ultimate total sacrifice provide us with the inspiration to deepen our dedication and commitment to the goals for which . . ."

When the mayor had finished, Reverend Jackson rose and delivered a response, probably more emotional than calculated, to the mayor's words. The minister was still wearing the green turtleneck, stained with blood, that he had worn the day before when he held his slain friend in his arms on the balcony of the Memphis motel where Dr. King was shot. He said:

"This blood is on the chest and hands of those who would not have welcomed him here yesterday. A fitting memorial to Dr. King would not be to sit here looking sad and pious and feeling bad, but to behave differently."

The concept that blacks must overcome fear and rid themselves of the sense of inferiority that is the heritage of 350 years of slavery and discrimination is one of the legacies of the minister's southern childhood.

"I remember how it was when I was a kid," he says. "We would say we didn't want to drink water because we weren't thirsty, or we didn't want to eat because we weren't hungry, or we didn't want to go to the movie theater because we didn't want to see the picture. Actually, we were lying because we were afraid. Dr. King's great contribution was to wake people up and make them face themselves. Once you make people face themselves their intelligence usually drives them to make the right decision."

Jesse Jackson was born on October 8, 1941, in Greenville, South Carolina. He knew poverty in his childhood, but never actual hunger. His parents had a combined income of thirty-five to forty dollars a week, his father working as a janitor and his mother as a maid in a local hospital. It was enough to keep a roof over the heads of the five Jackson children and provide them with the typical diet of southern blacks—grits or oatmeal for breakfast, corn bread and black-eyed peas and collard greens, chitterlings and neckbones, and in the Jacksons' case an abundant supply of chicken because they maintained their own chicken yard.

The family lived in a neighborhood typical of the black sections of most Deep South communities. It was a collection of unpainted, three-room "shotgun" houses, each with coal and wood bins underneath, an open toilet on the back porch, and a wash pot in the backyard. The houses were crowded so closely together that "you could stand on the front porch and holler three blocks up the street." That, in fact, was a favored means of communication, because scarcely anyone had a telephone.

The Jackson family, Mr. Jackson recalls with pleasure, was an exception. They did have a phone. It was a bit of good fortune for Jesse because it was used in emergencies by almost everyone in the neighborhood and he charged them five cents a call. His parents allowed him to keep the money and he used it to buy shoes, clothing, and holiday gifts.

Although the poverty of blacks in Greenville was no less cruel than that of millions of blacks who live in northern urban ghettos today, Jackson readily acknowledges that it was easier to endure.

"Whatever it lacked in material qualities, ours was a very stable home and a very loving home," he recalls. "My mother was a staunch churchgoer and so was my father.

Both sang in the choir. My sense of moral consciousness was developed in our home—an advantage that is denied many city children today.

"The whole community was poor, but we developed a lifestyle built around the Bible and, living in our own little ghetto, we didn't experience the pain that people feel now. This is not to say that the pain that's being felt now is not legitimate, but at that time we had become so accustomed to our inferior status that we had learned to live even within that. It has only been within the last ten years, as we began to break out and our psychological expansion took place and our aspirations increased, that we began to see the gap between where we were and where we ought to be. It is that new consciousness of the deprivation of black people relative to others in the society that has created the new tensions in the black community in the North as well as in the South.

"In Greenville we were poor financially but we were not poor psychologically or spiritually. Spiritually we were not poor because there was a lot of love in the house. Psychologically, the gap between us and other families was not so great as to make us feel poor."

There was also comfort and some sense of security in the fact that the residents of Greenville's black community were very close. There was little of the tension, hostility, and even fear of other blacks that often exists today in the northern ghettos to which many, like Mr. Jackson, later migrated.

"Every morning about six thirty you would find the adults sitting on the front porch drinking coffee and sharing coffee with others. Then about seven thirty most of them would go off down the street to catch the bus that took them to work at the white folks' houses.

"Somebody got sick or died and it was a big thing for the whole community, with everybody helping. Medical care was available—if we really needed it we could get it—but doctors and nurses were so scarce and the cost was so great and our expectations were so low that a lot of things people go to the doctor for now, we didn't even bother.

"I remember I had pneumonia and my grandmother broke it with an onion poultice. Home remedies were the thing and most people, when they got real sick, just stayed home and got well by taking onion tea and other remedies. There was a real sense of community there that you don't find among the wealthy in the exclusive suburbs, or even among the poor in our bigger cities."

Although Mr. Jackson did not sense it at the time, he realizes today that his motivation to lead his people from conditions of poverty and discrimination has its roots in experiences he had in Greenville as a child.

"I developed a strong resistance to white America's usurpation of the black community even then," he recalls. "All of those shotgun houses were owned by an old man named Mr. Hellum who used to come around on Saturday afternoon in his little old truck to collect the rent. He was white and he'd come around with his little book and those that didn't have the rent money would be running and hiding in the bushes and acting like they weren't home and he'd be chasing them to collect the rent. They were filled with fear, and I always resented that.

"But he wasn't the only one. There was the white insurance man coming around visiting people's houses all day, drinking coffee and collecting insurance. And white folks owned all the stores, just like they do here now.

"I had one very vivid experience with a white man who had a store on the corner. His name was Jack, and we used to run in there and play with him, so I always thought of him as a friend.

"The store was right in the middle of the black community, and one day I went in there and it was crowded, but I was in a hurry so I said, 'Jack, I got to go right away and I got to have some candy.'

"He was selling some bologna and didn't pay any attention to me so I said, 'Jack, I gotta go,' but he still didn't say anything.

"Finally I whistled at him, and do you know what he did? He whipped out a forty-five pistol and put it in my face and said, 'Goddamn you, don't you ever whistle at me no more as long as you live.'

"That store was full of black folks but not one of them moved and I didn't either.

"When I thought about that incident later I realized how much we all were conditioned by racism. My reaction was not a normal human reaction, but a black reaction in a white society. I didn't go and tell my daddy on Jack because I was afraid Jack would kill him, so I said nothing and internalized my fear and pain. That was my personal validation of white power. I couldn't tell my daddy on Jack but he could have told his on me."

The knowledge that he must accept an inferior status because of his blackness was impressed on Jesse in many other ways. One of the proud events of his childhood was one of Joe Louis's championship fights, which he and a group of other black children managed to hear on the radio by gathering on the sidewalk in front of a Greenville cigar store. Although Louis battered his white opponent unmercifully, Jesse and his friends stood there stolidly, not daring to show any emotion over a black man beating a white one because they knew it would anger the white shopkeeper and his friends.

As a child, Jesse accepted the inferior status that was accorded him, but even then he had an unspoken disdain for whites who claimed a superiority that was not really theirs.

"Most black people were never fooled by white folks," Reverend Jackson says. "They just accepted the alternatives under which they had to live because they were deficient in military, political, and economic power. But we were a long way from being fools, even then. I give black people a lot of credit for being wise to white folks all the time. It was only after Dr. King began to point out the need for blacks to stick together collectively, and after the success of that technique in the Montgomery movement, that black people began to vocalize what they had always felt. The Montgomery movement was like a jolt across the South, but the only thing really new about it was that the attitudes of black people were brought into the open. Black people had analyzed white people for a long time and they had analyzed them correctly."

Discrimination was present in many ways when young Jesse was growing up. He lived near the edge of a white community, and there was a white school within two blocks of his home. Jesse walked by it daily on his way to the black school, which was five or six miles away.

Although he subconsciously resented the discriminatory educational system that compelled him to walk that distance when there was a public school almost in his backyard, he found the walk exciting—he actually ran most of the way —and he enjoyed school. He was a good student, and the reward and punishment system used in the school provided him with ample recognition for his achievements. But even in the classroom the symptoms of racism were evident.

Reverend Jackson still recalls his second-grade geography book. One of the illustrations showed two boys standing back to back on the equator.

"There was John dressed in knickers and a British-type jacket. He was facing north. Facing south was Bumble, his hair so hard it seemed like the sunlight was bouncing off of it, and he didn't have anything but a little string tied around his middle. None of us wanted to be like Bumble."

It may have been his determination "not to be like Bumble," coupled with the strong moral influence in his home, that encouraged Jesse to work hard—in and out of school— to escape the poverty that surrounded him. Like most of the youngsters in the neighborhood, he gambled, but only a little.

"Momma didn't know it, didn't like it, didn't condone it," he recalls, "but all of us around there learned to play blackjack, learned to play what they call pitty-pat, used to play dirty hearts for money, played checkers, and everyone around there would shoot pool. I couldn't shoot very well, but was in the running for it. And on the corners, you know, we played those baseball tickets.

"Legitimate work was hard to come by, so many had to resort to some kind of hustle—bootleg liquor, selling baseball tickets, or anything else to make a buck. I was in that kind of environment, but I didn't get much involved in that. There was such a moral tension in my home between what I was doing and what my mother wanted me to do that I always kept a sense of balance. She had developed in me a certain conscience so that I always went to school every day and to church on Sunday."

Jesse got his first job when he was six years old, working on a truck hauling stove wood from a woodyard that his grandfather owned. Most of Greenville's poor had wood stoves—a matter of simple economics, because wood sold for twenty cents a basket and coal for a dollar a sack.

His grandfather employed workmen who went into the mountains for truckloads of slabs that were brought to the woodyard, cut into stove lengths, and then split. By the time he was eleven Jesse was in charge of the woodyard—his first experience in leadership—hiring and firing the men, collecting the money, and making up the payroll. At that age he had finished the fourth grade and was already better educated than any of the twenty men who worked in the place. Even his father had only completed the third grade. The one person in his family with more education was his mother, who had completed eleven years of school and had wanted to go on to college, but didn't have the money. Jesse didn't need much encouragement to continue his own education, but what he needed he got from his mother, to whom it was unthinkable that he would do anything else.

Reverend Jackson recalls that most of the young men in his neighborhood were fairly well dressed. For the most part they tried to dress as the white folks did, "because when we shined shoes or were caddying we admired their clothes so that's what we spent our money on.

"In fact, our dress was superior to most white kids' because we were dressing to compensate for some of the feelings of inferiority that we had. Kids still do that in the ghetto today. Even as a young boy, although my parents couldn't afford it, I was wearing Red Goose shoes, which was a name brand. Then sometimes we would go to the Opportunity Shop where white folks brought things they didn't want any more, and we got name-brand shoes there."

It was as the star athlete at the all-black Sterling High School that Jackson's black-white consciousness began to crystallize. The crosstown parallel of Sterling was Greenville High, which was all white, and Jackson's counterpart as the all-around white athlete was a lad named Dickie Dietz.

"I'll never forget," he says, "one night I ran three touchdowns and kicked an extra point. Nineteen points and we beat somebody twenty to six. Greenville High beat somebody seven to six and Dietz kicked an extra point. Next day there were big headlines in the paper, 'Dietz kicks extra point. Greenville wins.' Way down at the bottom of the page, 'Jackson makes three touchdowns. Sterling wins.' We lived with that kind of imbalance.

"The athletes used to follow each other because we were pretty objective about sports, regardless of black or white. If a white guy could really play ball, we admitted it. It wasn't any hang-up for us. In fact, a lot of us used to play ball together—white and black athletes—until the police would catch us and run us off. Sometimes we would go up to Greenville High and have some good games with the white boys. They'd come to our football games and we would go to theirs.

"In 1959 I went to a tryout camp—they used to let the black boys come, and they let me come to this one because I had developed quite a reputation. I was averaging about seventeen strikeouts a game. Two scouts came from the White Sox, basically to look at Dickie Dietz. He is now a catcher for the Giants, and even in high school he could hit a ball a mile.

"I got to the camp and I was the only black boy there. They asked me to pitch, and guess who was doing the hitting? Dickie Dietz! I struck him out three times; he foul-tipped one pitch. I guess they decided that I wasn't setting a good example for Dietz so they took me to one side and started talking to me about playing baseball for the White Sox and going to college in the off-season. Meanwhile, the Giants topped the White Sox and offered Dietz ninety-five thousand dollars. You got the picture? They offered the white boy nearly a hundred thousand and me, the black one, a chance to go to college in the off-season. That was my first real experience with the economic ways of white folks."

Mr. Jackson turned down the offer and accepted an athletic scholarship at the University of Illinois instead. He had earned letters in both baseball and football in high school and dreamed of going to college and becoming the first black quarterback. That dream was rudely shattered soon after his arrival at Illinois by an assistant coach, who told him that white boys were quarterbacks and black ones played halfback or end.

"I discovered that blacks were treated as badly at the University of Illinois as they were in the South, if not worse," Reverend Jackson says. "We were reduced to a sub-culture at Illinois. The annual interfraternity dance was the social event of the fall, only the three black fraternities weren't invited. My black friends and I were down at the

Veterans of Foreign Wars listening to forty-fives while the white folks were jumping to Lionel Hampton in the gym. Live."

But discrimination was something from which there was no escape. Jackson went home for the Christmas vacation and wanted to study while he was there, but couldn't use the public library in Greenville because he was black. He had to cut his vacation four days short and go back to Illinois to study.

In February of 1960, his freshman year at Illinois, students at North Carolina Agricultural and Technical Institute began a sit-down demonstration in Greensboro. They sat down at a counter in the local Woolworth store and ordered coffee, and when they were refused service they simply opened their books and began to study. Jackson saw the demonstration on television.

"Once an idea breaks loose in the universe anyone can grab it," Reverend Jackson says. "The idea was loose and in the next few weeks it was loose in Nashville, so by the time I got sick and tired of what was happening at Illinois and decided to transfer, North Carolina A. & T. was my choice because that was where the sit-ins started and it was the students who started them."

He enrolled at A. & T. on an athletic scholarship and there, with all the players black, he could be quarterback. He soon was "big man on the campus," a star athlete, honor student, national officer of his fraternity, and president of the student body. In the spring of 1963, while talking with some friends, he criticized the progress being made in the student sit-ins and was promptly challenged to lead them. Almost daily for ten months he led into downtown Greensboro the student marches that finally brought integration of the local theaters and eating places. In recognition of his efforts, Jackson was elected president of the newly formed North Carolina Intercollegiate Council on Human Rights.

Mr. Jackson majored in sociology at A. & T. and it was

there that he developed his interest in entering the ministry. It was an unlikely choice because, despite faithful church attendance as a child, traditional religion had depressed and frightened him. He felt that most of the ministers he had heard "preached doom and gloom and seemed to have given up on this world and focused their attention on the next one."

"For a long time I reacted negatively to the whole preaching thing because of my hang-up on traditional preaching and traditional preachers," the minister recalls. "But I had strong convictions about it and a lot of people used to tell me that I was smart and that I was going to preach, but I couldn't buy it because the moralistic straitjacket you had to walk in was inhuman.

"Still, I was very active in Sunday school and had a very strong church consciousness. Even with all the hell I was raising in college, I wound up being superintendent of the campus Sunday school. I was dean of pledges in the fraternity and I used to take all the little brothers to Sunday school—made them go every Sunday.

"After I got involved in the civil rights movement I began to talk with my president at that time, Dr. Sam Proctor, who was a theologian and a great preacher. I was having a hang-up on what 'the Call' was. I was looking for some cataclysmic religious experience, like I would wake up some night and be falling off a horse like Paul, or cutting flips in the middle of the air—shouting or something.

"Dr. Proctor told me that really the call was a certain consciousness that you have to serve a certain role or a certain mission, that perhaps I should go to the seminary just to try to understand what the ministry was all about. I went on a study mission for about a year, but after six months I found out I was at home. I never really looked back after that time—just kind of evolved into preaching."

The Reverend Mr. Jackson's view of religion differs from what he considers the traditional concept to be in that it is based on love rather than on guilt and fear. Rather than avoiding controversy and social conflicts, as most ministers are apt to do, he leads his followers into the heart of the battle, fighting injustice wherever it exists, much as Jesus did.

While at A. & T. participating in the sit-ins, Mr. Jackson met Jacqueline Lavinia Brown, and they were married during his senior year. His daughter, Santita, was born just as Jesse was being released from the Greensboro jail. He had been arrested for inciting a riot but the police couldn't make a case against him. When his first son, Jesse, Jr., was born, Jesse had just left a protest march with Dr. King in Selma, Alabama. He called home from a service station in Birmingham and learned that he had a son. The Jacksons' third child, Jonathan Luther, was born in Chicago, and Dr. King was his godfather.

After Reverend Jackson received his degree at A. & T. he went to Chicago and entered Chicago Theological Seminary. He completed two years there, but directed Operation Breadbasket at the same time. Last year he received an honorary doctorate from the seminary (he accepted the degree wearing the traditional robe, but removed it after the ceremony to receive congratulations in black Levis and a turtleneck shirt). His formal education, however, is not the education that gives him the most pride.

"Certainly my real education has been my association with Jim Farmer, Floyd McKissick, and Dr. King," he says. "That's where I got my doctorate degree in the school of life, and it has enabled me to traverse the whole black community and communicate with the people, which is a very vital need."

Today the militant Reverend Jackson traverses not only the black community in Chicago, but the innermost sanctums of corporate society, leading a struggle to increase black economic power. He had his baptism in Chicago during Dr. King's open housing marches through the city's

Marquette and Belmont-Cragin neighborhoods, when his head was anointed, not with water, but with an angry brick.

In recent years his vehicle has been Operation Breadbasket, the only financially independent program sponsored by the SCLC. The model for Breadbasket was the campaigns of Dr. Leon Sullivan, another imposing and courageous black preacher, in Philadelphia in the early 1960s. Sullivan, mobilizing black economic power in boycotts of white firms, spurred local business and industry to employ more blacks. He went on to found Opportunities Industrialization Centers across the nation. Their efforts to prepare young blacks for substantial careers are now supported by many of the same business organizations that were once the targets of Sullivan's wrath.

The objectives of Operation Breadbasket are to encourage blacks to support black-owned enterprises, and to compel white-owned enterprises that profit from black customers to provide equal employment opportunity for black workers and outlets for black-owned suppliers of goods and services.

Breadbasket, which uses the church to implement political, social, and economic programs, is an around-the-clock operation. Its mainspring is wound at eight o'clock each Saturday morning when the faithful gather at the Capitol Theater. The service is conducted with masterful showmanship, with jazzed-up old-time hymns sung by the Breadbasket Choir and the beat of the "now generation" represented by a thirteen-piece band.

The Reverend Mr. Jackson's theme song, as he strides slowly to the pulpit, is a boogaloo version of the swing tune, "Hard Times." This tune and another favorite, "Sometimes I Feel Like a Motherless Child," are almost unrecognizable in the style in which the band and choir do them, but they bring the audience to its feet in a frenzy of applause, dancing, and swaying rhythm.

By the time the vibrant young preacher, almost regal in a colorful dashiki, reaches the pulpit it seems that anything he could say must be an anticlimax, but the congregation is hushed when he begins to speak.

"Good morning, brothers and sisters," he begins. "Repeat after me:

"I am—Somebody!
I may be poor, but I am—Somebody!
I may be on welfare, but I am—Somebody!
I may be uneducated, but I am—Somebody!
I may be in jail, but I am—Somebody!
I am—Somebody!
I must be, I'm God's child.
I must be respected and protected.
I am black and I am beautiful!
I am—Somebody!
SOUL POWER!!!"

"I am somebody," the audience chants in response.

Reverend Jackson's sermons are not religious exhortations. Instead, he preaches about his concept of constructive black power, his formula for the achievement of black progress.

"One of the first things we must have is a common analysis of our situation, because all motion is not progress, and all black people doing things does not mean that we are going anyplace. Wild energy, sporadic energy that doesn't have any direction, is not of very much significance.

"We have to understand that we are already separate, for example—that we are separate and we didn't do the separating, white folks did the separating and we don't have the power to do the integrating. To understand that it is necessary for us to say that for our survival we are going to have to control the places where we live. That means that we are going to have to control ourselves economically, politically, psychologically, intellectually, culturally, and religiously. It means that we must strive to become

35

producers and not merely settle for being consumers. It means that we must recognize who our enemy is. Our enemies are those who usurp our jobs and who control us even though they do not live here—colonialism—there is no choice but to fight for survival.

"Rather than looking through the Yellow Pages we have to start looking through the black pages. The trouble is that Negroes have been programmed by white folks to believe their products are inferior. We've developed into a generation of Oreos—black on the outside, white on the inside."

One of the minister's more spectacular innovations has been the celebration of Black Christmas and Black Easter in Chicago's South and West Side ghettos. He says he conceived the idea of Black Easter because it is a holiday that most black people celebrate and he thinks they should celebrate it in ways more relevant to them. Also, he says, blacks need their own resurrection.

"We resurrected more than one hundred black heroes, more than one hundred black businesses, and more than one hundred thousand persons were involved. We renewed ourselves and not just our wardrobes. There was a very vibrant and powerful feeling in the conclusion that we were somebody. As long as people really feel that they can, they can. We may be in the slums but we are not of the slums, and as long as you are convinced of that you can fight and change things. *Slums are only bad when they get on the inside of you.*"

Reverend Jackson not only encourages the patronage of black businesses from his own pulpit, but has enlisted other black ministers to do the same from theirs. Congregations throughout the ghetto are exhorted to buy their milk from Joe Louis Milk Company, to make their sandwiches from Staff of Life wheat bread, and to use a variety of black-made products, ranging from Mumbo Barbecue Sauce to Swift Out Drain Opener and Afro Sheen for the hair.

Almost without exception these black companies have increased their sales, partly as a result of this clerical promotion of their wares and partly because of the pressure that Breadbasket has applied to white-owned chain stores to stock black products and display them favorably.

A typical pulpit sales pitch is one made by Mr. Jackson in behalf of Joe Louis Milk.

"Now, Joe Louis Milk does not come from a Negro cow," he tells his followers. "That milk has 400 USP like any other milk. It's written right there on the carton. Only difference is that your husband can make twelve thousand a year driving a truck for this company."

The results, from the viewpoint of the black-owned firms whose cause Reverend Jackson has espoused, have been spectacular. Sales of Joe Louis Milk have increased more than 20 percent since the Chicago ministers began their campaign. Similar results have been achieved for other black firms. Argia B, which makes Mumbo Barbecue Sauce, is now doing a six-figure annual business and the sauce has 15 percent of the Chicago market.

"If I thought we were just developing some more black capitalists with the same value system as white capitalists I'd drop the campaign," Mr. Jackson says. "The only thing dangerous about black power is that it might become like white power—compassionate toward machines, not people. What we need is white folks' technology and black folks' love."

Breadbasket's most spectacular successes have come in actions against large corporations that do business in the ghetto, validating Mr. Jackson's assertion that economic power is the most potent weapon of the disenfranchised.

"We have the power to cut the margin of profit on any product, Cadillacs or crackers," he says.

During its first fifteen months of operation, by picketing chain food stores and urging black customers to withhold their patronage, Mr. Jackson negotiated agreements with grocery stores, dairies, and soft drink manufacturers that yielded more than two thousand jobs for blacks and brought more than fifteen million dollars in annual income into the ghetto. The prime target of Breadbasket activity, which was organized at Jackson's Saturday morning meetings, was the Great Atlantic & Pacific Tea Company.

Capitulating in May, 1967, because of the economic loss incurred during Breadbasket's picketing of its forty Chicago ghetto food stores, A&P signed a precedent-shattering covenant with Operation Breadbasket. It pledged 770 jobs for blacks, appointment of twenty black store managers and twenty assistant managers, agreed to display the products of black manufacturers, use black scavengers and exterminators, use black contractors in ghetto store construction, and transfer some of A&P's banking business to two predominantly black-owned banks.

"A&P has merely contracted to do what it should have done yesterday," Mr. Jackson said at the time. "If this policy is carried out with honesty and determination A&P will cease to be the Man's store and will become our store. No longer will we allow the colonial powers—the white owners —to take profits and leave poverty, to take joy and leave sorrow, to take our sense of dignity and leave only despair. Ultimately the black ghetto must be controlled by black people."

The example of A&P's experience quickly brought other grocery chains into line. Operation Breadbasket then focused its attention on the dairies, reasoning that milk is perishable and dairies thus would be particularly vulnerable to the boycott technique. They were. From a hundred ghetto pulpits black ministers urged their congregations to boycott a dairy that had more than one hundred outlets in the ghetto. Within three days the dairy began negotiations with Breadbasket that ended with an agreement to employ forty-four blacks—20 percent of the firm's work force. Other dairies "heard the footsteps coming" and quickly followed suit.

In 1968, Reverend Jackson began to suspect that A&P was not living up to its original covenant. He promptly turned on the heat with a fourteen-week boycott and picketing that again brought the company to its knees. A new covenant was made that Operation Breadbasket intends to use as the model for negotiations with other white firms. The salient feature of the new agreement requires A&P to meet monthly with Breadbasket officials to report on its compliance with the commitments the company has made.

Breadbasket's leader insists that his strategy is not one of terror. "Our biggest concern," he says, "is to develop a relationship so that the company has respect for the consumer and the consumer will have respect for the company. As buying power among Negroes increases they will be able to spend more money, so it benefits both sides."

Although the efforts of Operation Breadbasket have largely been concentrated on improving the economic lot of blacks, Mr. Jackson's ultimate goal is one of shaping a class struggle in which the black and white poor of the nation will unite in efforts to better their condition.

"Poverty has no color," he says. "Politicians don't respect poor whites any more than they respect poor blacks. They have deliberately twisted the poverty issue, making it a black issue, turning anger against blacks instead of against the politicians where it belongs."

In the fall of 1969, while leading a protest aimed at forcing the construction labor unions to open up more jobs to black workers, Reverend Jackson was again arrested and carted off to jail. In order to dramatize the issue, he refused bail. The black minister, who is a victim of the sickle cell anemia prevalent among many Americans of African descent, is extremely susceptible to virus infections. He contracted pneumonia while in the House of Correction and was placed in a hospital bed.

From that vantage point he wrote an open letter, which was published in the Chicago newspapers, underscoring his desire to unite deprived blacks and whites in the achievement of social goals. The letter also reveals remarkable understanding of the hazards of polarization of racial attitudes present in black protests.

"We realize that our protest creates a counterprotest," Mr. Jackson wrote. "We seek jobs. The whites seek to maintain their jobs. It is understandable that they would want to remain employed. It should be just as understandable that we seek jobs which offer security, protection, opportunity, food, clothing, shelter, education, and the necessities of life. Both groups are frightened that they may be deprived of these necessities.

"White insecurity is expressed by excluding the outs and holding down the ratio of jobs. Blacks want unions opened up.

"Ironically, both groups are right. But each group is hardly able to see beyond achieving security for itself. Both think that the elimination of the other is the solution. The real solution is the expansion of the economy to the extent that it can absorb or employ both whites and blacks.

"The labor fight we are now engaged in threatens to further divide the poor black and the just recently removed poor white into greater racial polarity, with intensified racial antagonism. Each group develops programs of race glorification or chauvinism, locking up their jobs, schools, sons, daughters, families, and churches.

"This division of the races and the pending fight between the poor must be avoided. This horizontal fight between the have-nots must shift into a vertical fight—if there is to be a fight—between the have-nots and the haves.

"These fights between poor blacks and poor whites will inevitably occur if our economy maintains its present collision course. Everyone has a stake in this not occurring. But as long as there is surplus on one hand and starvation on the other, this gap will create tension in our nation. Our economy has the economic elasticity and capacity. Hopefully it will develop the moral capacity to adjust its priorities and make the dream of full employment a reality."

Mr. Jackson's concern about racial polarization causes him to view with some alarm the activities of young black leaders who advocate violence and separatism as the means of achieving black progress. Young blacks who have the will and the courage to assume leadership positions must, he believes, prepare themselves for the role if their efforts are to be enduring and effective.

Although critical of the quality of education available to blacks, Mr. Jackson still believes that "whatever education is available, one ought to get it."

"Our education down South in the best schools was even worse than the worst schools here in the North," he says. "Yet if one gets the fundamentals, the foundation of a good education, he can develop his own thought processes. One cannot give up on himself, even if he gives up on the educational system, even if he has to say 'I'm going to use the library and become self-educated.'

"One certainly cannot move to high levels of calculus unless he has mastered arithmetic and mathematics. One cannot move into high levels of speech training if he has never been trained in speech. One cannot convey certain technical tools to other black people if he does not have those tools himself.

"As for those who have leadership aspirations, one cannot lead where he does not go and he cannot teach what he does not know. Therefore, when you look around at the leaders in the civil rights movement who have sustained themselves over a period of years, you find that they were men who were trained. There was Frederick Douglass, a trained man; Nat Turner, a trained man; Booker Washington, a trained man; George Washington Carver, Du Bois, Walter White, Roy Wilkins, Whitney Young, Martin Luther King, Stokely Carmichael, Malcolm X, LeRoi Jones, Ron Karenga.

"All these men have wrestled with some of the great ideas of history and have more than common sense and soul sense. When you have been to school and have wrestled with these great ideas you are in a position to deny the validity of some of them and replace them with other ideas. But you can do that only because you really understand the ideas that have gone before.

"Dr. King couldn't have attacked the white churches as being corrupt and impotent if he hadn't possessed enough theology about the black and white churches to tell him what was relevant and what was not. Real education, not just mind training, is one of the real keys to leadership. Look at some of the revolutionaries—Castro, if that's your level of radicalism, a Ph.D.; Che Guevara, Ph.D.; Dr. King, Ph.D.; Ho Chi Minh, Ph.D.; Kenyatta, Nkrumah, Patrice Lumumba, all Ph.D.s.

"Plainly, not in the Ph.D. itself but in the hard work and mind development that went into getting it was the key to their longevity and the power to sustain themselves.

"Many of those with whom I started in school in 1960 dropped out to become active in the civil rights movement, but once they had exhausted all of their thoughts and ideas—thoughts and ideas that were limited because they had not wrestled with the great ideas of history—they just became bitter and frustrated. Some of them killed themselves and others went into the war on poverty and got jobs with the government and got all off the point.

"It is crucial to understand that mind development is of the very essence."

Two men in Reverend Jackson's life impressed him with the need to arm himself intellectually for leadership. The first was his professor of sociology at A. & T., Dr. Leonard Robinson, with whom Jackson talked often when he was involved in the Greensboro sit-downs.

"Dr. Robinson was the one who began to teach me the nature of revolutions and what it all meant. He didn't try to displace my own ideas. Instead, he forced me to read materials that would lead me inevitably to some of the positions that I now take. He was a Du Bois fanatic, so I read Du Bois extensively, along with Frederick Douglass, Booker T. Washington, Marcus Garvey, and many others.

"Then there was Dr. King. For me he has become a father image, a preacher image, and I guess the one I talk about least is the brother image; a very personal friend who would give me much advice, who used to talk with me about preparing myself for leadership, who indicated the kinds of books I ought to read, then talked with me and interpreted some of them.

"Dr. King loved black people, and he tried to make us stay true to the best in us despite our scars. But it is also true that he loved all people, and he tried to take the best in us and hold it up to the world to show how the world really ought to be.

"Then, of course, he died not on some lofty mountaintop, or in the court of some great ambassador. He died down South, in Memphis, fighting for garbage men.

"What a beautiful way to die!"

3

Anna Langford

Attorney for the Defense

If Anna Riggs Langford had fulfilled the expectations of most urban sociologists she would now be living in poverty as her mother and grandmother did. Anna's childhood circumstances were precisely those of an endless cycle of black mothers who have nothing to give their children but a legacy of poverty, hopelessness, and despair.

Instead, because of her unwavering determination and unflagging hope, the courageous girl broke out of the familiar pattern to become a remarkably successful adult. Today, she lives in relative comfort and affluence and has won distinction as one of Chicago's outstanding criminal lawyers. In a legal system dominated by men, that would be a significant achievement for any woman. It is a monumental one for a lady lawyer who also is black.

The recollection of her own childhood has had a profound influence on Mrs. Langford's career. She wages an unceasing battle against racial discrimination and much of her practice is in defense of young black activists who have had trouble with the law during protest demonstrations. The depth of her involvement in the civil rights movement is evident in the fact that the strategy for the late Dr. Martin Luther King's open housing marches in Chicago was planned in her living room in 1966.

Anna, a golden-skinned, brown-haired child, was born in Springfield, Ohio, fifty-two years ago. She was one of three children born of an interracial marriage. Her father died when she was nine months old. He left his white wife nothing but three hungry black children to raise.

No public assistance was available in Springfield forty years ago, and the untrained widow was forced to accept the most menial jobs as she struggled to keep food in the house and a roof over their heads. None of them lasted very long, for when her employers discovered that the petite white woman was the mother of three black children, she invariably lost her job.

This discrimination against her mother also brought to Anna her first awareness that society would treat her as an inferior because of her color. The revelation was doubly painful to the child because of the added realization that she was a handicap to her white mother because she was black.

At the time of her husband's death, Mrs. Riggs was living in a house owned by his father, who had recently remarried. Her inability to hold a job made it difficult for her to feed and clothe the children, much less pay the rent. She got farther and farther behind, and finally was told by Grandfather Riggs's new wife that she and the children had to move out.

The family moved into a decrepit shack which fronted on an alley—a situation common to many of Springfield's poor families in those days. The house was adjacent to that of Anna's white grandmother, whose economic circumstances were no better than theirs. Anna has little recollection of her early years in that alley home, where they remained until she was six years old. All that remains is the overall impression that they rarely had enough to eat and much of the time were cold.

Anna does recall vividly her disappointment when she could not enter school at the age of five. During that summer the black parents launched a campaign to have blacks hired to teach in Springfield's integrated schools. The Ku Klux Klan responded by marching through the streets and threatening violence with the result that all of Springfield's schools were closed for an entire year.

When Anna was six her mother remarried. The children's new stepfather, who was also black, took the family to his comfortable home, located in a neat and pleasant neighborhood in Loven, Ohio. For the first time in her young life Anna knew comfort and security, but it was to be very short-lived.

When Anna was nine her mother contracted peritonitis after giving birth to a son. The illness might not have been fatal, but when her husband sought to have her admitted to a hospital near Cincinnati they were turned away because he was black. Lacking adequate treatment, she died the next day.

Anna's stepfather did not feel that he could raise all of the children alone, so he kept the infant and sent his stepchildren back to Springfield to live with their white grandmother in the alley that they had left only three years before. They shared the tiny house with their grandmother's two sisters, one too ill to work, and the other—an alcoholic—unwilling to do so.

"Grandmother was the sole support of the household," Mrs. Langford says. "She worked for five different families as a domestic—12 hours a day, six days a week. The rent for our hovel was eight dollars a month. I remember the figure well because it was always our target. 'I've got six dollars; just have to get two dollars more to pay the rent,' grandmother would say."

Although the children were too young to be employed, they did what they could to supplement their grandmother's income. The prohibition laws were still in effect at that time, and the three youngsters scoured the streets and alleys looking for discarded whiskey bottles, which they could sell to the bootleggers for a penny apiece. Anna also capitalized on the taste of the black families in the neighborhood for wild greens. She picked them in nearby fields, soaked them in water overnight to increase their weight, and then sold them for ten cents a basket.

"I used the money to buy my school supplies and gym shoes," the lady lawyer recalls. "Most of the clothing we were able to get had been discarded by one of the families for whom grandmother worked. We never had anything new, except at Christmastime, when my uncle in Chicago would send some money, and we would go downtown to buy a few items of clothing. I remember very well the days when grandmother would come home with a bagful of shoes. Whichever shoes you could get your feet in—those were the shoes you wore. I still suffer from bad feet because of the ill-fitting shoes I wore as a child."

Anna's family went through the motions of celebrating every holiday, and she recalls that "Thanksgiving was always something special." Their Thanksgiving meal would have seemed ordinary to more affluent families, but to them it was a feast.

"We always managed to have a nice dinner on that day," Anna says. "We never had a turkey but we did have a couple of roasted chickens and we did always manage to have a full stomach. It was the one day of the year when we actually had enough to eat."

It was not uncommon for the home to be without food. The three Riggs children, who now called their grandmother "Mother," often waited at the window with their noses pressed against the pane, watching for mother to come down the alley with the leftovers from the table of the household in which she had worked that day. The quality and quantity varied, but anything she brought was always gratefully received.

Even when there was money for food, only the cheapest commodities were found on their table. The usual fare was dried beans, greens, potatoes, bologna, and liver pudding, which could be purchased for ten or fifteen cents a pound. They never had beef. The steaks they saw in the market were something to dream about, and even hamburger was beyond their means.

"Two things stand out most vividly in my mind about those terrible days," Mrs. Langford says. "In winter we were always cold, and all year long we were almost always hungry. I vowed then to my brother and sister—and to myself—that when I got older and was able to take care of myself I would never be cold and hungry again."

Anna began working toward her escape from poverty when she was ten. She found a job in the home of a dentist, taking care of the baby, doing housework, cooking, scrubbing floors. She did a woman's work, but they paid her only a dollar a week. The money was welcome, nevertheless, because it also helped to provide the supplies that she needed for school. This was of great importance to her because she was exceedingly fond of school and wanted to excel.

Excel she did, and in her classes Anna had few peers. She worked hard and led the class in most of her subjects because she was eager to learn and relished the attention she got because of her superior performance.

"I always made the honor roll," she recalls. "This set me apart from the others. It taught me that I could compete with all of the other children despite my economic status. The honors that I received also made me realize that there was something I could do to escape the poverty I was in and live a more rewarding life. I knew that the only way out was to get the best education that I could."

When Anna was eleven she won honorable mention in a citywide essay contest. Her subject was, "Why Fliers and Drivers Should Not Drink." It was a rather difficult subject for her to tackle, for she had never been in an airplane and they didn't own a car. The child was familiar, however, with the perils of excessive drinking, and the essay provided her with an opportunity to describe the tortures suffered by her alcoholic aunt.

Mrs. Langford still recalls the embarrassment she felt when she went to Springfield's Memorial Hall to receive her one dollar prize. She had no dress suitable for the occasion, and one had been improvised by cutting down a garment donated by one of her mother's friends.

"We had to wash and iron it because we couldn't afford to have it cleaned, and when we did all the pleats came out," she recalls. "It looked a fright—a big balloon all the way around—and I was most uncomfortable, but at least it was clean."

When Anna received the money her first thought was of her grandmother, and she rushed to the store to buy a pound of coffee. It was a remarkably unselfish gesture for a child who almost never enjoyed an ice cream cone or a candy bar.

"My grandmother loved coffee," Mrs. Langford explains. "She would buy a tiny bagful of it and boil each portion over and over until both the taste and the color were gone. This was the first full pound of coffee I had ever seen in our home."

Anna loved and respected her grandmother, and the child's interest in her schooling was carefully nurtured by the older woman. Despite her long and arduous hours of work each day, she always stayed up at night—sometimes until two o'clock in the morning—until Anna had finished her homework. Much of the time the grandmother would try to read, but her weary eyes would soon close, and she would fall asleep in her chair.

The moral support of her white grandmother may have been important in motivating Anna, for it would not have been surprising if she had been stigmatized into a feeling of inferiority and a fear of failure because of her race. All black children, whatever their economic circumstances, experience prejudice and discrimination, but Anna was exposed to them in three different forms.

"I realized as soon as I was able to leave our neighborhood and could scratch together enough money to see a movie that there were shows for white people and shows for us," she says. "And even then only a few theater balconies were open to blacks. You never saw a black person in a downtown restaurant or soda fountain, and we couldn't use the swimming pools at the YMCA. As I grew older I noticed that there were jobs for blacks and jobs for whites. The dirty, menial ones, of course, were set aside almost exclusively for us.

"That kind of discrimination was bad enough, but there was an equally sinister form of discrimination to which we were subjected because we were poor. This was practiced by the so-called upper strata of blacks who had made it—or thought they had. They looked down on those of us who lived on the other side of the tracks."

The third form of discrimination which Anna suffered was that inflicted by her black classmates because her mother was white. Often, when one of them had a birthday party she was not on the invitation list. It was not the children who discriminated—they were friendly at school—but when the party was at home their parents would not allow them to invite one of the Riggs children.

"I would be lying if I said it didn't hurt," the attorney says. "It did. But I soon developed a hard shell and was more determined than ever to excel in my studies. It was the only way open to me at that time to prove to them, and maybe even to myself, that I was just as good—if not better—than all of my classmates."

With the exception of one year, Anna was always on the honor roll. That exception is one that a less honest woman would conveniently forget, but Mrs. Langford finds the experience a useful object lesson for the young people she talks to today.

"When I was in the ninth grade I had been ill and was out of school for a while," she recalls. "Mr. Brinkman, my teacher, had always been very nice to me and I had always been on the honor roll.

"I returned to school just in time for the final exams. I was terribly afraid that I had missed so many classes that I would do badly in my exams and miss the honor roll, so I wrote out the answers on a newspaper in which my gym suit was wrapped.

"My first exam was in Mr. Brinkman's class, and I thought I was getting away with my deception until, suddenly, there he was, standing right over me. He took my test paper and walked to the front of the room where he tore it up in front of the entire class. It was a humiliating experience, and a costly one, but one which I deserved.

"Because I cheated I didn't make the honor roll, and the irony is that even without cheating I could have passed the exam with flying colors. I have never cheated again, from that day to this."

When Anna was twelve or thirteen she went to Chicago to live with a friend of her mother's—a young woman in her mid-twenties—who had taken an interest in the bright and ambitious young child. When the friend became financially unable to take care of her any longer, Anna packed all of her possessions in a cardboard suitcase and moved in with her uncle, James Riggs, who was one of Chicago's pioneer black real-estate men.

When the time came for Anna to enter high school, she discovered that the school district boundaries were arranged to exclude most black children from Hyde Park High School, the finest in the south side area. Determined to get the best education that she could, Anna registered at the Hyde Park school, giving as her residence the address of a friend who lived in that district. When she graduated in 1935 she had done so well that she was awarded a two-year college scholarship.

"When I was young I was always fascinated by the court-room scenes in movies when I was able to go," the attorney says. "Half fare for children was a nickel so we got to go once in a while. I always saw myself as the lawyer defending the poor, downtrodden defendant, and as a senior, in my autobiography, I said I wanted to become an attorney."

Unfortunately, Anna wasn't able to take advantage of the scholarship and begin the pursuit of a career in law because she had to help her aunt and uncle. When this was no longer necessary, she found a job as a clerk-typist in the office of the Illinois Secretary of State, utilizing the short-hand and typing she had learned in high school. Later she worked for the city election board.

In 1946, eleven years after graduating from high school, Mrs. Langford heard an address by Thurgood Marshall, who later became a justice of the United States Supreme Court, in which he reviewed the recent court decisions affecting civil rights. The eminent attorney described the long-range program of the National Association for the Advancement of Colored People to desegregate schools at all levels.

"It will be a long and painful struggle," Marshall said, "and many black lawyers will be needed in order to win."

Mrs. Langford was so inspired by Marshall's challenge that she decided, at the age of twenty-nine, to go to college and study law. Finding that she could continue working and attend a prelegal course at John Marshall College in Chicago at night, she enrolled in two classes and after taking her final examinations was dismayed to learn that she had failed in both. The dismayed student feared that her long absence from school was too great a handicap until she discovered that almost everyone had failed because the exams weren't written by those who taught the courses. In one class of forty-six, every student failed to pass the course.

Confident again that she could do the work, Anna transferred to Roosevelt University, which she attended at night for three years. She also enrolled in two summer schools, and had finished her prelegal training when she married Lawrence C. Langford, a City of Chicago electrician.

A year after her marriage Mrs. Langford enrolled in John Marshall Law School, and attended for a year until her son, Larry, Jr., was born. The blessed event caused another three-year lapse in her legal education which she spent fixing up a new home they had purchased, and getting acquainted with the new baby.

Her determination to become a lawyer did not diminish, however. She returned to John Marshall, and often stayed up until two o'clock in the morning to study, and then rose again at six to fix breakfast for her husband before she went off to school.

Mrs. Langford finished law school and passed the bar examinations in 1956. She was thirty-nine years old, but she still recalled her treatment at the hands of affluent blacks when she was a child and resolved that she would use her new talents to help those who lived in the ghetto, not to escape from them.

"I have a neighborhood office," she says, "not a plush office in the Loop. Many of my clients are referrals from the Legal Aid Society—people who make just a little too much to qualify for legal aid. They have a lot of trouble but no money to match it and are in desperate need of legal help."

Most of Mrs. Langford's cases are what one might expect from an impoverished ghetto clientele. Many are criminal, and others involve real-estate transactions and divorces.

"Once in a while," she says, "someone dies who has enough of something so that it is necessary to probate his estate."

The lady attorney says that she relies largely on volume to earn an adequate living, rather than on a few clients with a lot of money who could pay the fees that most lawyers expect.

"I may have to serve four or five clients in order to make the fee that another lawyer would make on one case of the same kind," she says. "I do an awful lot of work and much of it is on a low fee or no fee basis. But there is a need for this type of practice because you do have so many people just above the poverty line who cannot afford the expensive lawyers who practice downtown."

Since 1964 Mrs. Langford has been representing civil rights demonstrators in Mississippi and Chicago, usually without fees. She says she is motivated by the example of "the many young people who are willing to sacrifice their education, go to jail, and even to die, if necessary, in order to bring about equality." The lady lawyer represented many of those who participated in the rioting that followed the death of Dr. Martin Luther King, the demonstrations during the Democratic National Convention in Chicago, and subsequent events.

"Most white people blame the participants for these violent outbursts," Mrs. Langford protests, "when in fact it is their own society that is to blame. The riots that are occurring in the country were foreseeable and should have been foreseen. I recall at the time of the April, 1968, riots in Chicago, the *Daily Defender* printed an editorial that analyzed the causes of the rioting. They had published the same editorial seven years before, but society had done nothing to deal with the causal conditions in the years that intervened.

"Any time you put a whole lot of people in a depressed area, piled up on top of one another, and deny them the everyday rights they are entitled to under the Constitution, you should expect trouble. When you have merchants gouging blacks by selling them furniture that doesn't last long enough to pay the carrying charges on it, and setting wage assignments because they are one day late in their payments, it is not surprising that the day comes when this bottled-up hate and frustration is loosed."

Mrs. Langford says that black people must recognize that society will never yield to blacks their proper share of its fruits, that they will have to fight for that share every step of the way. She sees political power as a major part of the solution to the problems of blacks, and has actively sought political office herself in an effort to make her own voice heard.

In 1967, Mrs. Langford ran for alderman in Chicago's Sixteenth Ward and missed a runoff election by thirty-seven votes. The ward is primarily black, but the alderman and principal officeholders are white. When the polls closed on election day, Mrs. Langford and her workers were certain that she had polled enough votes to win a place in the runoff. Then she received a call from a volunteer worker in one of the precincts that the counting was being delayed and that something irregular appeared to be going on.

When the worker returned after making the phone call she was not allowed to reenter the polling place. The final count taken behind those locked doors showed Mrs. Langford the loser in that precinct by enough votes to defeat her chance to participate in the runoff. The day after the election she and her workers canvassed the precinct and received affidavits from dozens of registered voters who denied that they had voted in the election even though the records indicated that they had. She went to court, but the case was thrown out. Later, the machine politician who brought in the count from the disputed precinct was elevated to one of the top patronage jobs in the ward.

The attorney is not discouraged, however. She is busily reconstructing her volunteer political organization and plans to run again for alderman in 1971. There are many who are willing to bet that the results in that election will present a different story.

"If blacks are going to gain their proper place in society we must recognize that nobody is going to give us anything," Mrs. Langford says. "We cannot sit down at the bargaining table with love and hope on our side and all the power on the other. We have got to stick together and work together and gain power in any way that we can get it, politically or otherwise.

"I don't go as far as the youngsters who say, 'If we can't have it let's burn it down,' but there are times when I have been very discouraged and I can see how they feel. It just becomes a practical thing that they can't do it, but I can understand why they would want to.

"I think we have to understand that as a minority group we cannot have a successful revolution by going to war in the streets. I'm bourgeois enough to believe that we have to do it within the framework of the system, not through any extreme revolutionary measure."

Nevertheless, Mrs. Langford believes that change, if it comes, will occur because of the efforts of the militant young black people. Whether they are able to effect social changes which will lead to true equality of opportunity in the country depends, she says, on how well they prepare themselves for the role.

"My son is sixteen," she says, "and I don't tell him what to be, but just to *be*. I have tried to impress on him that there are no shortcuts to success, that whatever he does he first has to learn the hard way before he can learn the shortcuts.

"It goes without saying that every young person needs a good education, which is a prerequisite for just about everything he may want to do today. Even in inferior schools, there is a lot of self-training, through reading and extra study, that a youngster can do.

"It is also terribly important that young people not be discouraged because they are living in a deprived environment. They must tell themselves, as I did, that it doesn't have to last forever. If they don't do something about getting themselves out of it that is one sure way to perpetuate it."

"Just about every black person I know who has made it has had to face the same or similar obstacles," the brilliant defense attorney says. "Black kids have all these obstacles put in their paths—poverty, broken homes, discrimination —but they must not let the roadblocks get them down. Blacks have been overcoming them for many years, and the opportunity to do so today is better than it ever was before.

"Luck plays a definite part in the life of everyone, of course, but if a person fails to avail himself of all the opportunities at his disposal, then luck will have very little influence on his life. He will spend the rest of his days crying about how unlucky he is and how lucky someone else appears to be.

"The lucky person may have had a lucky opportunity, but you can rest assured that he was prepared to capitalize on the opportunity when Lady Luck smiled his way."

4

James Tilmon

The Sky Is No Limit

Jim Tilmon was eight years old when he decided what he wanted to be when he grew up. He was walking across the prairie near his hometown of Hominy, Oklahoma, kicking an occasional stone and daydreaming as children do, when he was alerted by the drone of distant engines. Looking up, he saw a silver speck in the distance and as it drew near he observed what looked like a huge bird with silver wings.

Awed and excited by his discovery, Jim ran all the way home and gasped out the exciting news to his family. His father, a schoolteacher with great patience, explained that the great silver thing was not a bird at all, but an airplane. It didn't fly by itself, he continued, but had a man at the controls called a pilot.

Jim listened eagerly as his father told him about flying and when the lecture ended said firmly, excitement still in his voice, "That's what I want to be when I grow up!"

For an eight-year-old to decide he wanted to become a pilot was not at all unusual. What made it exceptional in Jim's case was the improbability of it. In the 1930s and early forties all airline pilots were white. Jim Tilmon was black.

Happily, Jim did not know that there were no black pilots, and his father, after wrestling momentarily with his conscience, decided that he should not be disillusioned. Consequently, it was many years before Jim discovered that the deck was stacked against him, and by that time he had become so determined to fly that he refused to concede it was impossible. He simply decided that he would become the first *black* pilot, and from that moment on never lost sight of his goal.

Today, the handsome thirty-five-year-old flier is one of ten black men among the three thousand pilots who fly for American Airlines. Three or four days a week he folds his strapping six-foot-four-inch frame into the cockpit of a 727 Astrojet and flies the multimillion-dollar craft and its precious human cargo to cities all over the United States.

Between flights, back home in Chicago, Tilmon is known to millions as the host of the popular television show, "Our People," which is broadcast weekly on station WTTW-TV. The program is but one of many vehicles he employs in a continuing crusade to improve the lot of oppressed and impoverished Americans.

Tilmon is that rarity among blacks, a man who, although he lives in modestly comfortable affluence in a white suburb, has not turned his back on the problems of his black brothers in the urban ghetto. When he isn't flying or preparing for his television show, he is almost always busy doing something to further the progress of his race. He maintains a brutal schedule of personal appearances, mostly before youthful black audiences, and wears out more shoes than many Chicago cops while pounding the sidewalks to work with kids in that city's black neighborhoods. Now and then, when he needs to unwind, he dashes home to grab his clarinet and play a concert with the symphony orchestra in Evanston or Lake Forest, Illinois.

Tilmon believes passionately that the problems of poor

and deprived Americans, black or white, are not their problems alone.

"I haven't really made it, and neither has anyone else, as long as there is one hungry person in this country," he says. "No American can really be free until all Americans are free."

Any man with a schedule like Jim's would have reason to feel proud of himself, but if you ask the black pilot where he finds the energy and inspiration to do so much he looks surprised and replies:

"I don't really know how to answer that question because I have never felt that I was doing enough. I keep going seven days out of seven but I need eight. It often bothers me that I still take time out to do some personal things that I like to do. It makes me feel that I am shirking because the way things are in this country there really isn't any time.

"I have a television show that doesn't pay any money—just carfare, really—because I feel that I am able to communicate with my people, and help others to communicate, black to black. I talk with black kids, all over the country, about opportunity, but I try to do it in a realistic way—a way that they can trust. I try, by my own example, to show young people that there is a good reason to stay in school, to prepare yourself for the new opportunities that have opened up.

"That is really one of the most useful roles that I play as a black pilot. A white man described it to me once when he was trying to persuade me to give up an eight-year career in the Army and become a commercial pilot. He said, 'You have no idea what it would mean to me if I could see an airplane flying at twenty thousand feet and know that it might have your black face in it. It would make me feel more complete as an American citizen. If it would do that for me, imagine what it would do for your own people!'

"I never turn down an opportunity to do something meaningful. Sometimes it involves a small sacrifice, but most of the time I get far more than I give."

Jim, his wife Louise, and their two sons and one daughter live in a comfortable but unpretentious home on St. John's Avenue in Highland Park, Illinois, a suburb on Lake Michigan, north of Chicago. They moved into the suburb in 1965 in the wake of a furore that had developed when a black teacher in one of the local schools resigned because he couldn't obtain housing in the community. Mrs. Tilmon now teaches mathematics at Highland Park High School, where most of her pupils, like most of their neighbors, are white.

The affluent metropolitan neighborhood is in sharp contrast with the black rural communities in which Jim grew up. Hominy, where he was born, is as provincial as its name suggests. It is situated in the Osage country of northeastern Oklahoma, almost on the edge of the Indian reservation, and on those occasions when Jim left his black neighborhood to go shopping with his parents he saw more Indians on the street than he did white people.

"Throughout those years, and later when we moved to the all-black town of Boley, I never gave up the idea of being a pilot," Jim recalls, "but the reality of the obstacles involved hadn't reached me yet. I learned later that my parents were often asked why they didn't tell me that I couldn't be a pilot because I was black, but the fact that there were no black pilots had never occurred to me because I didn't *know* I was black. I guess I should say that I didn't know anyone else was white because I had never had any real contact with white people."

In Hominy, Jim attended Carver elementary school, where his father was principal. His mother, who taught the primary grades, was his first teacher. Although the economic circumstances of the Tilmon family were better than those of most of their neighbors, their income was barely adequate for their needs. Most black teachers in those postdepression days received meager salaries and Jim's parents were no exception, but they were fortunate in having a comfortable home provided for them.

The house was on the school campus, isolated from the black residential area several blocks away, so Jim had no real playmates during his early years except his older brother. After he discovered airplanes, he amused himself by building models with tissue paper and balsa wood and dreaming of the day when he would have a real airplane to fly.

It was when Jim was ten or eleven, after the family had moved to Boley so that his father could accept a position as superintendent of schools, that Jim began to develop an awareness of the fact that he was black. His parents had never discussed racial differences with him until one day when they were driving to Okemah, an all-white town a few miles down the road, to shop for things that couldn't be purchased in Boley.

"As we were driving along my dad said that there was a time when it was against the law for black people to get caught in Okemah after dark. You could be arrested, or beat up, or even worse. Although he hadn't said it was still true, that really frightened me. I had a horrifying mental image of us having a flat tire, or the car breaking down, and not being able to get out of Okemah before dark.

"What made it so terrifying was that in that car was everyone I loved, and to have anything happen to them was the worst thing I could imagine. I guess that was really when I first realized there was someone out there who was hostile, and from then on I began to identify a white person as being on the other side."

After three years in Boley the Tilmons moved to Sand Springs, Oklahoma, where Jim's parents still live. He was now in his early teens and by this time had discovered that the airlines did not employ black pilots, but the knowledge did not stifle his determination to fly. He continued to read everything he could find about aviation and spent the rest of his spare time building increasingly complex model airplanes, until his own bedroom was filled and they overflowed into the living room and dining room, where they were even suspended from the ceiling with pins and string.

As Jim grew older he became more and more aware of the racial discrimination that would plague him in the future but never, even subconsciously, did he concede that it could prevent him from reaching his goal.

"When I was a teen-ager I went to a department store one day and a kid who couldn't have been more than four or five—just a little kid—was sitting back to back with me in the shoe department. He was with his mother. I had barely sat down when he looked at me and gritted his teeth and said savagely, 'You nigger.' He said it with such venom that it frightened me because I wondered how this little kid could hate anything or anybody that much. He said it over and over again, 'You nigger, you nigger, you nigger,' and I kept waiting for his mother to tell him to stop, but she just sat there not saying a word. I finally moved.

"A little later we were on a train going from Oklahoma to Kansas City. I discovered that in Oklahoma they had curtains in the car that said 'Colored' on one side and 'White' on the other. Sometimes there was a whole coach for our people, and if a lot of black people were traveling some would have to stand up even though there were plenty of empty seats in the white coaches.

"My mother tried to explain this to me. She said, 'Some people have a lot of trouble trying to grow up, and the people who put those signs in here are like that. You have to be patient with them because they do not know how bad it is to make us suffer this way.'

"When you crossed the state line they removed the signs and the curtains and we could sit wherever we pleased. I just figured that the people in Kansas were a little more grown up."

When Jim finished high school he enrolled at Lincoln

University in Jefferson City, Missouri, where he majored in music education. He joined the Reserve Officers Training Corps because he knew that a commission in the military services would offer him the best opportunity to learn to fly. When he graduated in 1957 he got a reserve commission in the Army and entered the Corps of Engineers because he was told it would enhance his chances of being accepted for flight training.

Jim's first commanding officer was so prejudiced against blacks that when Tilmon reported for duty the officer barely spoke to him. He turned Jim over to the first sergeant and left the room. The black officer later learned that his CO had run all the way to the battalion commander's quarters, stormed in, and shouted, "What the hell do you mean sending me that nigger?" The senior officer threw the man out of his office, telling him he had better take the men who were sent to him, black or white, and that if he talked that way again he'd be court-martialed.

"The officer had to come back and accept me," Jim says. "He had no choice. But he made life miserable for me and I was pretty disillusioned. Everything he said to me was in a degrading tone, but I had to put up with it because he could ruin my career with one bad efficiency report.

"Then the guy decided to get married and he sent me a wedding invitation. It made me feel kind of good until he called me in a few days later and said, 'Jim, I sent you an invitation to the wedding, but of course you realize that we don't want you to come. We just wanted you to have an invitation anyway.' I gave the invitation back to him with a smile. The guy lives in this area now, and he called me one night after my TV show. Would you believe he thinks we should get together?"

Jim, then in his early twenties, endured a year under that officer's command, and says that it was only because he knew in his heart he was not inferior that he was able to put up with the man.

When Jim applied for flight school the officer again proved to be his nemesis. The officer was also a would-be pilot, but had been frustrated in his efforts to enter flight training. He had no intention of permitting a black subordinate to succeed where he had failed, so he recommended against Jim's acceptance. Fortunately, several other officers, who respected Jim and knew the conditions under which he had been working and the treatment he had received, were pulling for him. To his great delight his application came back in two weeks—approved.

"They wanted to see me do something that my CO couldn't do," Jim says. "Gosh, what a fantastic party we had the night my orders came through, all on those other guys. I learned that all along, without being aware of it, I had friends running interference for me. They had really kept this guy from ruining my career. When I left I threw a party for the whole battalion. I don't remember how much it cost but it was a whole bundle of bread and it was worth every penny!

"At flight school I discovered that there were only two black students per class and I was told that they never graduated more than one. They said one of us would be gone within two weeks and sure enough, two weeks later, the other guy got thrown out. I felt sorry for him but not sorry enough to wish it had been me. It was a great day when I finally got my wings!"

After flight training Jim went to Fort Belvoir, Virginia, to work on research and development and attend career school. He wanted to become a nuclear deployment officer but discrimination again reared its head. The officer who made the selection told Jim his math scores weren't good enough and that he didn't have the aptitude to make it through school. Jim knew the officer had no valid basis for this judgment and proved it by threatening to take his case all the way to the Pentagon or even to the president. The officer was furious but he admitted Jim to the course.

Tilmon removed any doubt about his aptitude by finishing second in a class of sixty. For once in his life he didn't fret over being number two, because the number-one man was a nuclear physicist from Massachusetts Institute of Technology. Jim was one of three graduates selected to teach a course in structural analysis for fallout protection to men who were being trained to build shelters for civilian protection.

The big turning point in Jim's career came when, after having flown small planes and helicopters with the Corps of Engineers in Germany, he decided to leave the Army. Although he had won virtually all the awards given to non-combat soldiers, he was restless because he did not feel that the Army was giving him the opportunity to make the most of his own life or to contribute enough to improving the lives of other blacks.

"I went to my commanding officer," Jim recalls, "and told him what I was thinking. I asked him if he knew whether there was any mission in sight for our outfit—I was then in the Eleventh Air Assault Division—and he said he didn't know. Then he spent an hour cussing me out. He told me what he was going to do to me for even thinking about getting out of the Army. At that moment I knew I didn't ever want to go to war with him."

Looking for further guidance, Tilmon flew to Washington for a talk with Colonel John C. H. Lee, who had been his commanding officer in Germany. Colonel Lee is a direct descendant of General Robert E. Lee, and Jim considers him to be the epitome of an army officer.

"I used to work three days without sleeping for Colonel Lee," Jim says, "and if there was a man I had to die next to as a soldier, he would be the man. When I told him what was on my mind he didn't even hesitate over his reply. He looked at me and said, 'Jim, by all means get out. You not only have your own life to live, but your people need you.'

"That was all I needed to hear. I applied to get out of the Army on July 8, 1965. Ironically, on July 28 the president announced that my unit was going to be renamed the First Cavalry Division and shipped to Vietnam. My footlocker was already on its way there, but I was a civilian again."

Tilmon gave up about fifteen thousand dollars a year when he left the Army, without having any real notion of what he was going to do. But he had not lost his determination to fly, so he began applying to the commercial airlines for a job as a pilot. At the time very few blacks had been employed by the airlines because, Tilmon says, "they were scared to death they would lose passengers," but the color barrier had been broken, so his objective was not as impossible as it once had seemed.

Tilmon's first choice was a job with American Airlines, but he also wanted to live in Tulsa and, because American was closing its Tulsa base, he decided to apply to all the airlines. He tried about a dozen of them and discovered that many were checking on applications from military pilots to determine whether they were black or white. Only three were willing to talk to him. One told him he was "a cinch for a job," but he never heard from them again.

"Another airline went through the same act with several black pilots," Jim says. "They told you that you were hired and then stalled around until you got a job with somebody else. Then they sent you a wire telling you to report to them. They were so obvious about it that they sent my wire to the American Airlines Training Center.

"American, when I talked to them, was very discouraging. I didn't have any jet time, had spent much of my time flying helicopters, and had flown in the Army rather than the Air Force. They hadn't had any experience with army pilots and were disturbed because I had only done about five hours of instrument flying. I really wasn't ready for American, and they told me so. They were very honest.

"I guess I wouldn't be flying yet if the man in charge of flight operations for American hadn't taken a look at the applications and decided that there was nothing wrong with an army pilot. It was a great day at our house when he not only decided to hire five army pilots, but also took one who was black."

Tilmon is a first officer with American, flying as a copilot, and is one of about fifty black pilots now flying with the major airlines. American doesn't hire copilots as such, but hires men it knows will make captain as soon as they have enough seniority. It will be another year or two before Tilmon takes command of an airplane.

During an average week Jim flies three and a half days. He bids for the trip sequences he wants and the monthly schedules are awarded on the basis of seniority. This gives him the opportunity to try to arrange his schedules so that they fit in with his heavy off-duty program. Although he started out, during his first probationary year, earning only sixty-five hundred dollars, his income increased substantially during his second year when he began getting paid for each minute of flying time. His salary that year was between thirteen and fourteen thousand dollars. He now makes about eighteen thousand a year, and when he makes captain it will increase to twenty-five thousand. With enough seniority, and flying heavier and faster airplanes, he will be able to make forty thousand dollars a year or more.

But money isn't everything. Jim's experience as one of the few black pilots in the nation has also been spiritually rewarding.

"I never see jealousy or envy in the faces of black people I meet when I am in uniform," Tilmon says. "I always see pride, pride that one of their own has made it with the airlines. They even stop me now and then to tell me so.

"I remember the first time I pulled into the gate at Washington National airport. Two black guys in the ground crew were standing there looking at me in astonishment. I couldn't open the window to say anything to them, so I gave them the closed fist—the black power symbol. They not only answered in kind, but did it with enthusiasm and smiles of approval that let me know we had communicated. It was a beautiful experience."

The black pilot is a staunch advocate of the black power concept, contending that it is nothing more than "good old American arrogance" being exercised by black people in their own behalf. He maintains that some of the wars we have fought, the imposition of our language and customs on other peoples, and white treatment of black people in America are all examples of "white power" except that we have never called it that.

"Just as white power did, black power must begin with an economic base and then move into other areas such as politics," Jim says. "I don't look at black power as being anything but positive. It is the first cry after the birth of a child that will grow into manhood and full citizenship for black people in America. Without an aggressive approach no other group of Americans has ever achieved full-fledged citizenship. Blacks have never exercised this strategy because they did not come here in immigrant status. Most of them came here as slaves. The time is ripe, and we now have the chance to gain a proud place in American society in spite of the odds."

Tilmon concedes that the achievement of black economic and political power means that black people must become more militant and that many whites regard black militance as a dangerously threatening attitude. He disagrees.

"To me militance is a beautiful thing, which will improve the health and increase the wealth of the nation, not something to be feared and condemned," he says. "Being militant in this country simply means that we, as members of the American family, have the right to damn that family for its own good. Militance must be distinguished from forms of aggression that are nothing more than violence for the sake of violence alone.

"A militant person, and I consider myself one, is simply a person who is not satisfied with the way things are, and has the will and the guts to say so and try to do something about it. That's not bad, it's good, because a satisfied person may be the most dangerous person there is. Even if we didn't have racial problems we would need militants to keep the country moving, to keep it alive and healthy, to continually question our system for its own sake."

Jim believes that this is what the sincere young people on the college campuses are doing—questioning the system for its own sake. He says he doesn't support violence as a solution, but can understand that there may be times when, having exhausted all other means of communication, the students will conclude that no other way is left.

"Adults in this country, comfortable and secure in their affluence, will never understand these kids unless they try to understand them in their own frame of reference," Jim says. "These aren't just kids going to school. In their own terms they are adults living in a war-torn country. My age group, and most of those who are older, and most of the professors and instructors who are not themselves hiding from the draft are not living in a war-torn country. We are living in a peacetime economy that is being very good to us, and to us there is no war.

"Why can't we understand that these kids who are subject to the draft, who know they may have to go off and get shot up in Vietnam, are in a war environment and have every right to behave like people in a country at war? We ask them to die for a cause that many of our own national leaders tell them is wrong, and then can't understand why they are restless, and concerned about the political directions the country is taking, and frustrated because their point of view isn't even represented. They have the right to die but they don't have the right to vote."

Jim considers it a healthy sign that young people are becoming adults much earlier today, and considers it encouraging that being an adult is coming to mean—as they see it—being a full-fledged American citizen who "gives a damn about which way the country goes, and how people are treated, and the kind of controls that will dominate their lives, and the amount of vertical mobility they will have within the total society."

"Unless you want to preserve the status quo so that you can profit at the expense of somebody else, there is nothing so frightening about that," Tilmon says. "Far from being distressed by these kids, I am amazed and heartened by their courage and conviction and determination. I am encouraged by their concern for their education, even to the extent of being willing to sacrifice it, if necessary, in order to make it meaningful for those who are to follow. Our universities, which should have been the leaders of progressive thought in our country, have been dragging their feet. They deal with the young people of America, but they haven't bothered to keep up with them."

Although Tilmon has great empathy with the young people who are trying to improve the American system, he has no sympathy for those who waste their time and energy trying to overturn it. Blacks in particular, he believes, have no time for anything but "making it," and he is convinced that the capitalist system, more than any others, offers the vertical mobility and the natural incentives that will enable them to do so. The challenge, he says, is to make the system work for everyone, not to destroy it.

When he talks to young black audiences, Tilmon points out that whites also have had problems within our system, but he maintains that blacks have a greater opportunity than white people to find a way around the problems.

"We have the ingenuity that is common to black people in this country," he tells the youngsters. "We have the ingenuity that keeps you alive when you don't have three square meals a day; the ingenuity that kept many of us in the schoolroom when we had no good rationale for staying in school; the ingenuity that enabled many black people to make history in this country in spite of the odds.

"If we will just take a little piece of that and arm ourselves with skill and knowledge, nothing can stop us. I see that kind of talent among so many of our young people— talent so great you want to burst with pride. Unfortunately, much of it is being wasted because the kids don't have any goals, or think they have more time than they do, or relieve their tensions in violent and destructive ways.

"There is nothing to gain by making yourself visible in a negative way—cussing people out, breaking windows, or doing harm to somebody. Like Bobby Rush of the Black Panthers said to me once, 'Those are little victories, if they are victories at all. Most of the time they are not even that, and who needs that kind of victory? It doesn't do you any good and it certainly doesn't do black people any good.'"

Tilmon says that young blacks should be militant, but in practical ways that promise some end result that will be profitable for black people. Instead of wasting their energy in pointless violence, he urges black youngsters to get rid of their tensions in ways that will bring results.

"We must spend every ounce of energy that we can muster preparing ourselves so that we can outdo that white guy," Tilmon says. "We've got to get educated, make the ballot box work for us, know when to complain and who to complain to, know where the shortcuts are that will help us make it.

"One of our greatest advantages as black people is that we have always had to go uphill, and that builds strong legs. While the Man is coasting we may be able to run right by him. We've got to spend all of our time making this system work for us because when we do there won't ever be any reason for any of us ever to want to be white.

"Wouldn't it be funny if we got to the place where we became the elite minority that ran this country? We have more potential for doing that, if all of our young black people really apply themselves, than any of us has yet dared to imagine!"

Tilmon doesn't talk much to his own children about their role in society because he feels that they are learning from experience and will be guided by his example. He takes them with him whenever possible, particularly on his visits to Chicago's black neighborhoods, because he doesn't want their suburban existence to cause them to lose their identity as black people.

He teaches them, as his mother taught him, the need to be patient—"patient with the man who doesn't know that his own mental and social growth has been stunted by prejudice, patient enough to understand that that man has a serious problem to live with."

When talking to other youngsters the black pilot does not conceal his own belief that white Americans will never accept black people in the way that they accept other people. He says, in fact, that there is so much hate white-to-white in America that he is not sure he wants to be a part of it.

He talks a great deal about the breadth of opportunities that have opened up for black people in recent years, but says the opportunities are not there because white people like, understand, or want to accept black people, but rather because they need their talents.

"You have to develop your talents to the point where you can be proud of them yourself and maintain confidence not just in your blackness alone, but in the fact that you are truly prepared," Tilmon tells his youthful audiences. "If you do that you will have no problem arming yourself with the kind of determination that will say to you what my determination was able to say to me.

" 'Black is beautiful' is a phrase that is perhaps the most important black people have uttered since I have been alive—indeed, in the history of black people in America. But it is an empty, shallow, meaningless group of words if that is all we have to say.

"Black can only be truly beautiful if we make ourselves understand the true meaning of beauty. We are beautiful when we are smart enough to understand the tools and technology and methodology of making power work for us.

"We are beautiful when we are knowledgeable enough to understand our own good points and the other man's limitations, and expect no more of him than he is capable of giving, but demand that.

"We are beautiful when we make our homes, our community, our city, our nation better places to live in—not just for us but for everybody.

"We are beautiful as long as we maintain the human dignity and integrity to resolve that we will never perpetrate on another group of people the offenses that have been inflicted on us.

"We are beautiful, in short, when we are honest with ourselves and with those around us about every phase and facet of our blackness. That is the basis of my patriotism. That is what keeps me from flying for SAS and trying to live in Scandinavia.

"I am not willing to sit around and wave the flag with the ridiculous .ideology that America is beautiful just for the sake of itself. And if I won't do that for America, which I swore to die for during the eight years I spent in uniform, then I certainly won't do it for a slogan like 'black is beautiful' unless black people in this country are willing to put real meaning into that phrase."

5

James Brown

The Sound of Soul

Even in America, long hailed as the land of opportunity, James Brown's meteoric rise from rags to riches is almost too much to believe.

Black grade-school dropouts with prison records just don't escape the slums of Augusta, Georgia, to sing for the president in the White House. They don't buy radio stations as though they were popcorn, own their own record companies, or flit around the country in their own private jets, and certainly they don't gross three million dollars in a single year.

They don't, but James Brown does.

When people talk about children who were born in poverty and deprivation, James Brown is what they are talking about. He was nine years old before he owned a suit of underwear that wasn't labeled "Pillsbury's Best—XXXX." Most of the time he had only one pair of shoes and went barefoot all week so that he could save them for Sunday. When he got hungry, which was much of the time, he usually had to sing for his supper.

Brown was born in Augusta in 1933 in the very depths of the Great Depression. The year is remembered with anguish by many older adults as the one during which all the banks were closed, but that disaster was of little consequence to Brown's parents. They had never had enough money to put any in a bank.

Actually, the Depression itself didn't make much difference to them. To those already struggling at the subsistence level, an economic crisis means only that they go on subsisting or cease to subsist. Fortunately for folk-rock music lovers, and for James, the Browns went on subsisting.

The black soul singer remembers living in several different houses as a child, because his father never could manage to keep a place of his own. Until James got big enough to earn the seven-dollar monthly rent, the Browns faced a seemingly endless succession of eviction notices, if the landlord bothered with that formality and didn't just throw them out in the street.

Throughout his childhood, James lived in flimsy unpainted shacks, without window sashes or glass, plumbing or electricity. On cold or rainy days the window openings were sealed with sagging wooden doors and the interior of the house, shabby even when the sun streamed in, became a dark and dismal cell. Thus, home for James was not a place to live but a place to avoid, and avoid it he did, as much as he could.

"We usually had a fireplace, but no stove or heater," Brown recalls. "Eventually we got an old cookstove and my mother took in washing and ironing for other people to help keep the family going. She had one of those irons that you put on the coals to get it hot."

Despite their hopeless poverty the Browns were never on welfare. James says it wasn't because they weren't eligible, or even because his parents didn't want to accept charity. His father just didn't know how to go about it. He had left school in the second grade and Mrs. Brown in the fifth—a level of education that their son says left them functionally illiterate and unable to cope with the complexities of the world.

"It was impossible for them to know many things because

their scope was limited," Brown says. "We lived in the ghetto. Completely in the ghetto. We never had chicken or steak or pork chops, but survived on the most basic foods. The only meat we knew was fatback, smoked bacon, and chitterlings.

"My only clothes were hand-me-downs, and not from an older brother, because I was the only child. I was nine years old before I got my first suit of underwear out of a store. My mother and my aunt made our underwear out of flour sacks after they had used the flour.

"I only had one pair of shoes. Went barefoot until Sunday in order to make them last so I would have them to wear to church. Never had more than one suit and that usually came from the pawn shop and was altered to fit. Sort of. I probably wouldn't have had the suit or shoes if it hadn't been for church. My parents were very religious so we faithfully attended the Baptist church.

"We hardly knew about doctors. Used home remedies most of the time, and that was a bad thing. I have heart trouble today because of having rheumatic fever and not taking care of it right. I got it when I was very small and had it bad when I was about five and about seven. That's what happens in the South. Once you have had it, every year you have a relapse. I never went to a doctor, just had sassafras tea and all kinds of home remedies."

Brown recalls that the highest wage earned by anyone in his neighborhood was about twenty dollars a week. His father, a turpentiner who chipped trees to get the tar that was distilled to make turpentine, made even less than that.

The singer has no recollection of childhood fun and games. Like many ghetto children today, he grew old in a hurry and was street-wise at a very early age. He worked hard as a child, and it took all the ingenuity he could muster to find enough money to sustain himself and pay the rent. He picked up coal along the railroad tracks, selling some of it for pennies and taking the rest home to warm his own house against the chilly Georgia nights. He ran errands for anyone who would pay him, delivered groceries, medicines, and even telegrams.

When he could find no other chores to do he shined shoes on the steps of a local radio station (he owns it today), and in his early teens he worked until eleven o'clock at night racking balls and sweeping out in an Augusta pool hall.

Whenever possible James tried to earn extra money for the family by singing and dancing, the two things he most enjoyed doing. He danced and sang on street corners, or for the National Guardsmen who camped in town, hoping someone would toss him a nickel or a dime. He had to dance long and fast to earn seven dollars a month, a nickel at a time, and that may account for the lightning feet and enormous endurance he displays on the stage today. During the few years he spent in school he even took over the auditorium and collected ten cents a head from kids who wanted to watch him dance and sing. They didn't know it at the time, but they got quite a bargain, because Brown can now gross as much as one hundred thousand dollars in a single night.

Brown says that his parents were "unaware" as far as his education was concerned, but an elderly aunt did teach him to read and write. That paid off when he finally enrolled in school at the age of eight, because he was able to cram seven grades into five years of attendance before finally dropping out of school for good. He liked school, was extremely bright, and received a great deal of encouragement from one of his teachers. Her name was Laura Garvin, and he never forgot her. She is working as an announcer in his Augusta radio station today.

Paradoxically, the event that diverted Brown from a life of poverty, frustration, and hopelessness was getting arrested and sent to jail. After years of struggling for nickels and dimes in legitimate but degrading ways, he became determined to get something more from life. He made the mistake of trying to get it from someone else—without his consent—and was sentenced to four years in a juvenile institution for breaking and entering and stealing a car.

Several months of confinement gave Brown time to consider the error of his ways, and he concluded that he had the talent and the intelligence to be something better than a delinquent. He decided to get himself out of there and took a typically direct approach.

"I wrote the parole board that I was a kid from a poverty-stricken family, a family that was unaware, that really didn't know about life because they had never had a life themselves," he recalls. "I told them I wanted to get out and do something for myself as a man. They let me out right away. It had never happened before."

When he left the institution Brown had served eleven months of his four-year term. He resolved that it was the last he would ever see of the inside of a jail.

Calling on the experience he had gained during years of singing for his supper, Brown formed a trio. He had long been annoyed by synthetic British imitations of the big-beat soul sounds, which he regarded as the exclusive property of southern blacks, so he adopted the authentic style as his own. It is a highly personalized blending of the blues and the gospel forms he had learned in church as a child. His style caught on almost immediately, and when he was "discovered" during a recording session at a Macon, Georgia, radio station in 1956 he was thankful that, years before, he had saved his shoes so he could learn the songs sung in church.

The James Brown song and dance style is so personal, so emotional, so powerful and pervasive, that it almost defies description. For most of the soul brothers in his audiences his performances are an emotional experience that can't be described because it has to be lived. Brown's press agent, who is a leading authority on his employer and the fans who have declared allegiance to him, has described the singer in these words:

"James Brown is the greatest showman on the stage. From Harlem's Apollo Theater to Evansville, Indiana, or Africa's Ivory Coast—in any town or city in America where soul is king—James Brown will explode regularly for improbable fees. When 'Mr. Dynamite' is in town, money is only 'bread' and all that's important is a clear view of the leader working, falling to his knees and biting off the words to 'It's a Man's World' and 'I Can't Stand Myself.'

"James Brown in person is a one-man multitude, crowding the stage with a traffic jam of steps, cradling the mike—and singing. Grandmothers weep, women call out to him or stand with their faces buried in their hands. The men clap against the beat and with it, screaming, 'Yeah, yeah.' Two drummers thunder home the soul sound. Brown drops to one knee. 'Please, please, please,' he begs, he screams on his knees.

"The crowd curls over the tops of the chairs, like a tidal wave, roaring. Then two aides come from the wings and, draping a velvet cape over his shoulders, help him slowly, painfully off stage. The wave cries out, 'James, James,' but the Maestro is gone and the show is over."

Press agents are renowned for their talent for exaggeration, and one must feel sympathy for Brown's, because, hard as he tries, he can't overstate the impact the singer makes on his audiences. Brown's popularity is reflected in the affluence that has come his way since he won his first gold-plated platter.

He lives in a $250,000 mansion in Queens, New York, with his wife, Dierdre, and their three children, but he maintains such a demanding schedule that he sees little of them. They have two Cadillacs, a Rolls-Royce, a Mark III, a Toronado, and a Rambler, but rarely does Brown have the opportunity to drive them.

The singer says he never has an off day in the sense that

he isn't doing anything. When not performing or promoting records, he is checking on his radio stations (he owns two and will soon have five) and a vast array of other enterprises.

Brown's many business and charitable activities are carried on through two umbrella corporations, James Brown Productions and James Brown Enterprises, which employ more than one hundred people in New York, Cincinnati, Los Angeles, Detroit, and Macon. He has a publishing firm, Try Me Music, and a production company, Fair Deal Records; he recently launched Gold Platter restaurants, a chain of carry-out places specializing in chicken and soul food, and has plans under way for a chain of hotels. He has also invested heavily in apartment houses and a variety of securities.

In 1965, with a forty-man group known as the James Brown Show, the singer was on the road for 340 days, during which he grossed more than a million dollars. But that was only a warm-up. Three years later Brown cruised the country five days a week in his speedy Lear Jet and made 335 appearances, most of them one-nighters. His gross was estimated at *three* million dollars, about two hundred and fifty thousand of it take-home pay. *Ebony* magazine called him "the biggest draw in America."

What the take is from his many other enterprises is anybody's guess—he hasn't revealed it—but it has to be astronomic. He has recorded twenty-five singles, which have averaged more than a half-million copies each in sales. Every one of his last ten records has sold more than a million copies. Small wonder that he now concedes he is a multimillionaire.

Brown isn't the only one who benefits from his frenzied activity. He supports both his parents, who are now separated. His list of charities includes several colleges, churches, and schools. In 1969 he turned down one hundred thousand dollars in bookings in order to tour Japan and Vietnam. He

lost seven pounds during one exhausting midday performance at Tan Son Nhut air base, outside of Saigon. He
appeared there on a day when the city suffered one of
the heaviest Vietcong rocket attacks of the war. Ten rockets
dropped inside the air base, but it didn't stop the singer
from giving two performances there.

The recollection of his own unhappy childhood remains
vividly with Brown, and he is involved in many activities
that he hopes will help other youngsters in similar circumstances. In 1968 these efforts brought him the annual Hu-
manitarian Award of B'nai B'rith.

During the riots that followed the death of Martin Luther
King, Brown got on radio and television in both Washington
and Boston to try to "cool it" by urging his soul brothers
to get off the streets. He has supplied millions of children
with James Brown "Stay in School" buttons in a campaign
to keep ghetto children from dropping out of school.

A good part of Brown's driving ambition—one of the
things that keeps him going at a killing pace even though
he has all the money he will ever need—is his desire to
prove to black people, by his own example, "that they can
do it."

"I'm trying to build their courage, motivate them to want
to do, motivate them to independence," Brown says. "It
will help the black man more than anything else in the
world to feel that he is equal to any other man, and he
ought to, because he is."

The old-fashioned values are often shot down by the
younger generation in the battle that is raging at Generation
Gap. There may be some message for them in the response
you get when you ask the idol of the Soul Set what he
thinks they should do to get the most from their lives. His
notions sound suspiciously like those parents have been giving their children ever since Samson launched the crew
cut fad by letting Delilah cut his hair.

"The only things you get out of life are things that you

get for yourself," Brown says. "Opportunities today are much better, but opportunities are made. They don't just open up by themselves. A lot of black kids don't get anywhere because they never try.

"Black people have had a bad deal from white people in this country, but it's not only what the white man did to the black man, it is also what the black man failed to do for himself. Don't just be black and proud and leave it at that. Be a man or a woman—that's what counts. Do something for yourself, something on your own. Be determined to pay your own way.

"You know, the Boy Scouts are one of the finest organizations in the world. They're trying to motivate independence—the will to do, to want, to know what it means to need, and the will to supply that need honestly.

"Be willing to look for help, and don't be too proud to take good advice from anyone, whether he is black or white. Surviving is a hard thing, and if your family can't take care of you, can't help you, find somebody or some agency that will. If you don't know what to do, sit down with your teacher or your principal and tell him the truth and he'll tell you what to do. You're bound to get in trouble if no one will take care of you and you're too young to take care of yourself.

"Stay in school, because unless you get a good education you'll never be your own man. Work so you can have your own money for the things you want to do. Don't earn a hundred dollars and spend a hundred and ten. Spend eighty-five and save fifteen, so you start getting a reserve going for you. The average black man doesn't do that. He lives from day to day. You've got to plan for tomorrow and save, and invest, because unless you have ownership you will never have black power.

"Let your word be your bond. Be right, be dignified, be cool, be all the things it takes to be a nice person. And always remember that verse in the Bible that I think is the most important of all of them. It is a good philosophy: 'Do unto others as you would have them do unto you.'"

Brown's words may sound trite, but they are trite only because they have been said to and heeded by most of the people who have succeeded in the world. Brown learned from bitter experience what it takes to make it and what it takes to fail. He learned that there are no cheap and easy shortcuts to success in life, that the shortcuts lead to jail.

6

Richard Hatcher

Gary's Black Mayor

Dick Hatcher's first real job, as a high school boy in Michigan City, Indiana, was in the kitchen of a local restaurant, washing an endless stream of dirty dishes that poured in from the dining room out front. The young athlete got the job because he was a valued member of the high school football team, and local merchants made it a practice to provide employment for members of the squad who were in need of financial help.

The lad's duties kept him in the kitchen most of the time, so he had little opportunity to observe the nature of the restaurant's clientele. But one day he happened to be in the dining room when a couple who were traveling on the highway came in and sat down. They were black.

The customers sat patiently for some time, but the waitresses studiously ignored them. Finally Hatcher asked one of the girls why nobody was serving the black couple. She didn't reply, but went to the cashier's station at the front of the restaurant and spoke to the manager. A moment later she came back and told the couple that she could serve them if they would go in the kitchen to eat. It was Hatcher's first realization that he was working in a restaurant that discriminated against blacks.

"I was so burned up I tore off my apron, threw it at the

manager, told him that I quit, and walked out of there," Hatcher recalls. "When I got home I told my father about it, and he made me sit down while he talked to me.

"He said something to me at that time that I'll never forget. He said: 'There are things that happen that I don't like and that you don't like, but there are many times when, in order to get what you want, you have to take unpleasant things. Once you get what you want you don't have to take them anymore.'

"The owner of the restaurant kept calling. I guess he was upset and worried about getting some bad publicity because I was fairly well known as a member of the football team. Meanwhile, my father kept trying to persuade me to go back to work there. Finally, I asked him how I could possibly go on working in a place where they wouldn't even serve *us*. He said, 'You need this job because you are trying to do something for yourself. You should work for that and this other thing is going to get straightened out.'

"So I went back, oddly enough, and I worked in the restaurant for the rest of the year. I saved my money and the next fall I went off to Indiana University for my first year in college. When I came home in the summer of 1952 I got some friends together and we went into that restaurant and staged the first sit-in in Michigan City's history. We sat there for seven nights in a row, filling up all the seats, and finally the restaurant owner capitulated and began serving blacks.

"The interesting thing is that the guy who owned that restaurant is still a friend. He now has a whole chain of restaurants, so he realizes that he didn't go bankrupt because we made him start serving blacks, and he still talks about how a black dishwasher changed the course of his life."

Hatcher says that he "had to swallow a lot of crow" to go back to his job in the restaurant, but that today he is glad he did. Because he took his father's advice to bide his time until he had prepared himself to bargain from a position of strength, he integrated the restaurant and solved the problem that was disturbing him. More important, he got the educational foundation that enabled him to become the first black mayor in the sixty-one-year history of Gary, Indiana.

Hatcher, now thirty-six, was born at the bottom of the Depression on the west side of Michigan City, but moved while still an infant to an area called "The Patch." It was the city's worst slum. The family moved because his father, who had worked for many years for the Pullman Standard Company, lost his job when the Depression began, and couldn't find another. He was able to support his family only by pushing a junk cart through the alleys and collecting paper, cardboard, and scrap metal which he could sell.

"The Patch was a classic slum in every sense of the word," Hatcher says. "It did not have paved streets—just dirt roads —and most of the houses fronted on alleys and were in various stages of disrepair and deterioration. There wasn't a lawn in the neighborhood, so until I was nine or ten I didn't even know about grass."

The Hatcher family numbered fourteen children, but only seven of them survived. They lived in The Patch until Richard was a junior in high school and fifteen years old. Of two homes they had there, the one that he remembers best was a large house, gray in color "because it hadn't been painted for years" and heated by two coal stoves, one upstairs and one down.

"Sometimes the only way we could get coal for fuel was by going into coal cars on the railroad tracks across the street and filling sacks that we dragged home," Hatcher recalls grimly. "I suppose that was stealing and I suppose we did quite a lot of that during those days.

"The police were always on our back, and we didn't necessarily have to do anything to incite their displeasure. I had friends who were involved in things—I was involved in things. We used to go downtown with big overcoats and steal from the dime stores. It wasn't right, but it was hard to be honest when you didn't have anything and were very young and so very poor. The police were always in our neighborhood because they figured something was going to be happening there. I remember one time they were after a gang stealing bicycles—just routine, but they came to our house and searched.

"I never went to jail—I don't know why—I guess I just never got caught. But it was just normal, if you were standing on a street corner, for a policeman to come by and tell you to get off the street and call you a black so-and-so."

Hatcher says he was very much aware of the fact that they were poor, almost from the time that he can remember anything. For a time he slept in the same bed with three of his brothers and sisters, because there weren't enough beds to go around.

"In the winter there were never enough covers," Hatcher says, shivering a bit at the recollection. "I still remember how unhappy we would be when my father would tell us that we had to let the fire go down at night because otherwise there wouldn't be enough coal the next day."

Hatcher says that the staple of their diet was beans, and they rarely had meat more than once a week. Often the main meal of the day was biscuits and syrup and nothing else. The family was never on welfare, but Hatcher does recall that on Saturdays his father picked up food baskets containing canned fruit and dried milk.

"I remember many days when I didn't go to school because I didn't have shoes," he recalls. "More often, when I did go, I remember how embarrassed I was because the shoes had holes in them. With three older brothers, I was always wearing hand-me-downs, and I recall the great thrill and delight I felt when I got the first suit I ever owned. I must have been sixteen years old."

The mayor says that he can't recall a time in his childhood when he got sick enough so that his parents felt they could spare the money to call a doctor. His mother died of cancer, after refusing for a long time to see a doctor, and Hatcher says that he is sure she would have suffered less if she had received proper medical care. The most obvious result of lack of attention in those years, however, was the fact that the family couldn't afford the services of a dentist. As a consequence, all of the Hatcher children have had trouble with their teeth.

Hatcher's recollections of The Patch are vivid and unpleasant.

"Our house was located a block away from a company that processed animal hair," he says, wincing at the thought. "Until I was eleven I didn't know that the smell from that factory wasn't the way things smelled everywhere. My mother worked there in one of the rooms where they had to braid the hair. I used to go down to run errands for her and the other women who worked there, and it was a very filthy place as I recall it.

"The neighborhood had no playgrounds, swings, slides, or anything like that. The only bright light in the whole area was a Methodist church that had a small gymnasium attached to it. It was called the 'Elite Youth Center,' and was like a neighborhood house, and I used to go there after school to play basketball and Ping-Pong after I had finished my chores.

"The director of the center was a man named Charles Wescott, and I suspect he is responsible for getting more boys started on the right track than even he is aware. You could talk to him, and I guess he was about the only thing between us and everything bad when we were outside our home. He did a tremendous job and, in fact, he's still there and still doing the same kind of work."

Hatcher says that he rose to his present position, despite the poverty and deprivation of his childhood, because of "the tremendous drive in the family"—his father's desire to see his children become somebody, his willingness to work and sacrifice to achieve that for them, and the strong religious atmosphere in the home.

"I think the reason I don't drink at all is because I never saw a bottle of liquor in the house," Hatcher says. "And I think another beautiful thing that really gave me a lot of basic strength was the fact that I never, ever heard my father or mother say a single angry word to one another. They must have argued, but if they did it was behind closed doors. Even though we were very poor it was a very rich home as I look back at it. There was a kind of basic religious undergirding that made up for the lack of material things.

"My mother belonged to the Sanctified Church—the Church of God in Christ—and she used to take me there. My father belonged to another church—he was a Baptist. We went to church at all hours of the day, and there was always a strong religious atmosphere in the home. When my mother died my father took us to his church, and I was baptized a Baptist. I now belong to St. Timothy's church here in Gary, but I am still a Baptist by affiliation.

"I have some rather strong feelings about the kind of strength and support that one draws from a belief in God, and that belief has always served me very well."

Hatcher's father, who worked until recent years as a laborer in a foundry, had very little formal education. He went only to the third grade, and he could not read or write, but was good at arithmetic. Hatcher says he had a "kind of simple philosophy" that if a man worked hard and always paid his bills that was very important, because then you could get credit when you needed it. Even if it meant going hungry he always paid his bills on time.

"If I were to try to look to the single person who provided me with the kind of continuous encouragement, support, and inspiration that is so essential to every young person, it would just have to be my father," Hatcher says.

"His feeling was that although he had not had an education he would live for his children to get that education."

Considering their extreme poverty, the father was remarkably successful in achieving his goal. Of the seven children in his family who lived, every one graduated from high school, two graduated from college, and one—Richard —went on to graduate school. Two of his sisters went to business college, another is manager of a housing project in Muskegon Heights, Michigan, and another is on the staff of the township trustees' office in Michigan City.

Hatcher says he believes that many of the youngsters who "get off on the wrong track today" do so because they lack the kind of guidance and inspiration that his father gave him. He cites, as an example, an event which occurred when he was eleven or twelve, at a time when his father was the treasurer of the Baptist church.

"On Sunday Dad used to bring home large sums of change from the collection and he used to hide this money," Hatcher recalls. "One day I found it, and reached in and got a handful of coins, which I took to school and used to treat all of my classmates.

"My father found out immediately that the money was missing, so he got all of us kids together and asked which of us took it. My immediate instinct was to deny taking it, but then he said something that made me change my mind.

"He said, "You know, whoever tells me the truth will not get whipped, but if I find out who did it and they haven't told me I am going to whip them.' I remember that I confessed immediately, and he didn't whip me, and from that point on I never lied to my father again about anything. He had simply given me the feeling that I could tell him the truth without expecting horrible consequences.

"It was little things like that over the years that inspired me to hope that I could become half the man that he is. If I can I will be pretty well satisfied with myself, because he is quite a man."

Hatcher says that as a result of his father's inspiration and encouragement he has always, from his earliest recollection, wanted to make something of himself and get out of the poverty-stricken environment he was in.

"I remember seeing the well-dressed kids in school and hoping that some day I could look like them," he says. "But not having decent clothes wasn't the worst thing. I remember how it bothered me that I was always behind on the book rental money, so that when I finally got the books I was two or three weeks behind the rest of the class and always trying to catch up.

"Often, the extracurricular activities at the school called for bringing a dollar or two dollars, and I couldn't participate because we just didn't have it. In grade school, I wanted to play the violin until I found out how much they cost, so then I decided to play the piano.

"I remember several false alarms when my father found out about someone across town who had a piano for sale, but he always came back and said it had been sold to somebody else. As a result, I never got the piano, but I enrolled for piano lessons in school, anyway. They were free, and for a long time I was able to fool the teacher into believing that I had a piano to practice on at home. She finally found out that I didn't and made arrangements for me to practice on the piano at school during the lunch hour. So I was able to continue taking piano lessons all the way through grade school.

"I recall how determined I was to go to college, which was pretty ridiculous under the circumstances, but I guess that young people are more optimistic than anyone else. During my junior year in high school we were finally able to move out of The Patch into a better house, and I remember that I graduated from high school feeling that now that we were in a decent house I would be able to go to college. It was that very night that my father told me there wasn't any money to do it with.

"I told him that one way or another I was going to go on to school, and he got me a job at Pullman, where he was working again. I saved some money that summer, but it still wasn't enough, so they took up a collection at church and raised between three and four hundred dollars toward my tuition. I got a small athletic scholarship at Indiana University, and also a job waiting on tables in the dining hall, and putting all those things together I was able to get through the first year. After that, it was just a matter of doing essentially the same thing."

Hatcher graduated from Indiana University where he majored in economics and government and became an impressive public speaker. He decided that he wanted a career in law, so he went on to Valparaiso University where he attended classes from 8:30 to 3:30 and then worked in a hospital from 4 P.M. to midnight to pay his way through school. He graduated with honors in criminal law in 1959.

When he had passed the bar examination, Hatcher began the practice of law in East Chicago Heights, and soon developed a thriving practice. In 1961 he was appointed to the staff of the Lake County Prosecuting Attorney, and his performance in Criminal Court led to his appointment as deputy prosecutor. He resigned that post to run for the City Council in Gary, Indiana, in 1963.

Gary was a grimy, corrupt, crime-ridden city with a population slightly under two hundred thousand, which had been established more than sixty years earlier to house workers employed by United States Steel. Its black population, many of them descendants of workers whom the company had brought in years ago to break a strike, had increased to 55 percent. Yet, although more than half of the population was black, most of them were compressed into 6.6 square miles of a city that covers more than 56 square miles overall.

Gary had long been under the control of an entrenched Democratic machine that had allowed crime to flourish while doing nothing to improve the community or correct the miserable conditions under which many of its citizens lived. Hatcher, defying the machine, ran as an independent Democratic candidate. He received the most votes ever polled by a candidate for councilman-at-large in the history of the city. Within a year the bright, able young councilman had been elected president of the council—the first freshman member ever to achieve that honor, and the youngest ever elected to the office.

"The primary problem at that time was that there was a very strong political machine in control of Gary as well as Lake County," Hatcher says. "They were not especially anxious to welcome any new aspirants for office who had no past history of working with them. We had a number of wonderful volunteers—people who worked very hard. They didn't know all the political rules so they just worked with people and we won the election."

In 1967, unable to prod the city administration to do anything to correct the deplorable conditions that existed in Gary, Hatcher decided to run for mayor. Critics of his campaign said he was not qualified because he was too young and had not lived in Gary long enough.

"My answer on both counts was that I got here as fast as I could," he says.

It was a difficult campaign. Hatcher had no money, and he experienced great difficulty in getting people to support him because nobody thought he had a ghost of a chance. He couldn't buy the billboards and advertising space that the other candidates had, and tried to make up for it by attending house parties, going from door to door, and organizing volunteer groups to work closely with the people. He was successful in the primary election only because the other two candidates in the primary divided the anti-Negro vote.

"Ordinarily, in Gary, if a person wins the Democratic primary that's tantamount to election because the Democratic party then steps in with the assistance and campaign funds necessary to win," Hatcher says. "In my case that didn't happen because the Democratic county chairman did not feel I was flexible enough, or willing to play ball with many of the party leaders. Initially, he cut us off from all financial support.

"We had to ask people all over the country to contribute to the campaign because that was the only way we could keep it going. Harry Belafonte came to Gary to do a benefit concert which raised some money to keep us going. Julian Bond came and spoke at a fund-raising dinner, and we were getting that kind of help from all over the country.

"When the county chairman saw that the withdrawal of party support was not stopping us he dropped his neutral position and began openly to attack me. He implied that I was a Communist. He said I was an extremist because I refused to disavow Rap Brown, Stokely Carmichael, and even Marlon Brando. He wanted me to denounce Marlon Brando because he had signed a peace document that appeared in the London *Times* demanding an end to the war in Vietnam.

"My refusal to denounce any of these people really irritated him and others in the party. I had not only the Republican party working full time against me but many in the Democratic party also working full time against me. Fortunately, the people—the little people—were there, and they gave us the help and support that we needed."

At one point in the campaign the campaign treasury was disastrously low, and money was desperately needed for advertising and literature to offset the combined opposition of the Republicans and many of Hatcher's own party. Against the advice of many of his associates, he ran a $6,906 ad in the *New York Times* and an $860 ad in the *Gary Post-Tribune,* appealing for funds. At least three people mortgaged their homes to help pay for the ads, and when the bills had been paid there was only fourteen dollars left in the campaign treasury.

"For God's Sake, Let's Get Ourselves Together," the ad's headline screamed to its readers. Above an appeal for an end to bigotry, ignorance, and violence was a photograph of a white policeman clubbing a black.

Within a week about nine thousand dollars in small contributions poured into Gary from all over the nation, more than enough to pay for the ad. By October, more than sixty thousand dollars had been contributed, and the campaign was solvent again.

Although Hatcher had a good deal of white support, he found many white audiences wary of him, if not actually hostile. He sometimes shocked them by saying:

"I know you haven't heard a word I said. All you see in front of you is black. But if, by some miracle, race was ruled out and I and my opponent were considered only on qualifications, this election wouldn't even be close. All my opponent talks about is that he comes from an old family, long established in Gary. He says he's been in the furniture business for forty-seven years. I want to see that he stays there."

About two weeks before the election Hatcher felt that he had a good chance to win. Then he discovered that there was a scheme under way to steal the election. Officials who opposed the black candidate had added thousands of false and fictitious names to the voting rolls in the white community, and planned to vote those names on election day. Meanwhile, they had arbitrarily removed from the rolls the names of about five thousand blacks. Some twenty to thirty thousand votes against Hatcher would be counted even before the polls opened on election day.

"Fortunately, as the result of the conscience and honesty of a precinct committeewoman who knew about it, and came and told me of the plot, we were able to stop it,"

Hatcher says. "We went into federal court and got a re-
straining order against the county chairman preventing
him from carrying out the scheme and preventing all of
those involved from carrying it out. As a result they were
not able to vote the false names, and the black people
whose names had been removed from the rolls were—by
direct order of the judge—allowed to go in and vote. This
enabled us to come out with a very narrow victory—about
eighteen hundred votes. If the scheme had worked it
wouldn't even have been close."

Hatcher has now been the first black mayor of Gary for
nearly two years. He has launched many new programs,
but says they are "not going to solve all of the problems
next year or the year after that."

Half of Gary's thirty department heads are now black,
and the city has more black school principals than there
are in the city of Chicago. About half of the teachers are
black, almost the percentage found among the pupils, sixty
percent of whom are black. The police force has been increased from 274 men to 331, and one hundred of them,
instead of forty as before, are black. The city government,
Hatcher feels, now more accurately represents the population of Gary.

"I feel that we are making a good deal of progress,"
Hatcher says, "although much of it is like an iceberg in
that it is largely hidden. It takes time to gear up programs
to provide employment, housing and other needs. But slums
are being torn down, new housing *is* being built, people
are finishing training and working on jobs. Last year for
the first time in twenty years we got some low-income
housing built in our city. I think that we have taken some
very important steps in solving some of the problems that
we have. I also would be the first to say that we still have
a long way to go, but I feel we are headed in the right
direction."

One of Hatcher's principal achievements has been to make

some inroads into organized crime in the city. Major crime in the city has declined, an effective police-community relations program has been launched, and much of the policy racket, gambling, and prostitution has been driven out of Gary.

Recalling his own childhood experience of living in the dirt and mud of Michigan City's Patch, Hatcher has prodded the city to build three large new parks, two of which are in the heart of the ghetto. For the first time, he says, people in that congested part of the city will have some greenery, and a place to take their children.

Hatcher sees improvement in the attitude of white society in America toward racial problems, but says that changes are being made "much too slowly, grudgingly, inch by inch."

"There is a real question in my mind as to whether the larger society is going to be willing to make the kinds of radical changes that are necessary and to make them in time to avoid a complete and total disaster for our country," he says. "I think that is the real question, and right now I wouldn't lay odds that it will.

"We hear a great deal of talk about cutting back on programs that were inadequate to begin with. The 'War on Poverty' was really a kind of a skirmish and if we are talking about de-escalating from that we are talking about going backward instead of moving forward.

"One way or another this country has to decide whether it wants to build hydrogen bombs, tanks that won't work, planes that won't fly—spend billions of dollars on a plane and it won't fly—or whether we are going to take that money and use it on people, to help people.

"I think an excellent example was the hospital strike in Charleston, South Carolina. It has been pointed out that the government of South Carolina spent eight thousand dollars a day to maintain troops in that area to suppress people who were protesting in behalf of their rights. If they took that same eight thousand dollars and gave it to the people, they wouldn't be protesting."

Hatcher says he believes that if the poor and the black are to make progress in America they must organize politically and support candidates for office who are concerned with solving their problems, not simply with perpetuating themselves in office. He notes that other ethnic groups, through political action, have carved a slice of the political and economic pie for themselves. As an example, he points to Chicago, where a Polish population of less than a million sustains four of its group in Congress, while more than a million blacks have elected only one of their own.

"Someone in Chicago has a piece of the power that blacks should have," the black mayor says. "One of the things black people must do is recognize who the real enemy is and stop fighting with each other. You keep hearing uncomplimentary remarks about militants, moderates, Uncle Toms. As long as there is more than one person in the world you are going to have varying shades of opinion, and I think it is important that black people recognize that they can ill afford the luxury of fighting each other.

"I won't debate whether Roy Wilkins, as opposed to Eldridge Cleaver, has the right idea. I'm not interested in debating that. What I will say, though, is that each of them is making a contribution and whether we agree with their message or not the fact is that they are trying to accomplish the same goals. That's what is important."

Hatcher says he thinks "it is interesting" that the campus militants are demanding more black studies courses, and attempting to define a black heritage that they can be proud of, but says he feels that the real test of their militance will come when they get back to their own communities.

"Are they still going to be as concerned and militant in demanding full and equal justice for all the people then?" he asks. "That will be the real test of their militancy.

"It seems to me that the college campus is an isolated situation, but the real world is the slums and the hearts of cities where people are still suffering from rats and roaches and everything else that goes with them. The real question is whether those militants are going to be as insistent about seeing that the slums are torn down and that people in them be given the same opportunities that they will have and that everyone else has."

Mayor Hatcher, whose twenty thousand dollar annual salary is twelve thousand dollars less than he made during his last year in private law practice, lives in a small house in an all-black neighborhood on the east side of Gary. He is a bachelor, but says he has a big family to worry about —the young children of Gary.

"I have a great time going to the schools and talking to them about their problems," Hatcher says. "I think my election has given those youngsters something to really identify with—to realize that they have come of age as people and have a stake in the city of Gary."

Hatcher says his real concern when he considers the future of black Americans is not with the advice he can give the children, but how he can motivate their parents.

"If they don't have all the material things there is still much that they can do for their children that may not make up entirely, but will help," the young mayor says. "It is important that parents make children feel needed and wanted, and that they encourage them to go to school and go with them to church every Sunday.

"Throughout my life I have had the wonderful benefit of having a father who was always with me and behind me— who always supported me in the things that I wanted to do. That was extremely important to me because it gave me self-confidence. There were other individuals who also pitched in and gave me a helping hand and developed in me a kind of confidence in myself.

"I know it isn't easy for many parents to sound encouraging to their children when they are having such a desperate struggle just to survive. But any time they can give their youngsters some encouragement it will pay off, as it has paid off with me."

7

Frederic Davison

Making It in the Military

Colonel Frederic E. Davison was on an operation west of
Saigon on July 15, 1968, "flushing some VC out of a pine-
apple plantation," when he received a call ordering him
to report to the headquarters of the U.S. Army in Vietnam.

Davison was acting commander of the 199th Light Infantry Brigade at the time, filling in for Brigadier General
Franklin Davis, who was in the United States on leave. The
operation was routine—nothing like the bloody Tet offensive through which he had led the same outfit a few months
before. Davison reacted to the summons with the apprehension common to professional soldiers summoned from on
high, wondering what kind of trouble the brass was cooking up for him this time. But, because he *was* a well-disci-
plined soldier, he acted on the orders without delay. Leaping
into a helicopter, he was whisked off to the USARV headquarters, only twenty-five minutes away.

When he arrived, Davison was told to report to the office
of General Richard A. Edwards, the deputy chief of staff
for personnel and administration. The general greeted him
nonchalantly, offered him a chair, and then exchanged
pleasantries for ten minutes while Davison waited patiently
across the desk, wondering what was coming next. Finally,

General Edwards reached into a drawer, pulled out a tele-
type message, and asked:

"Have you seen this?"

Davison replied that he hadn't, and Edwards handed
the sheet of paper to him. The general grinned broadly as
he watched the expression on the colonel's face change
from one of apprehension, to astonishment, to sheer delight
as he read and then slowly re-read the message: the White
House had nominated him for promotion to Brigadier General in the Army of the United States.

Tidings such as those would have delighted any officer
in the Army, but to Davison they could only have been
surpassed by an announcement that Hanoi had decided to
end the war in Vietnam. They meant that he was assured
of becoming the third black general in the history of the
United States. In nearly three hundred years of U.S. military history silver stars had been pinned to the shoulders
of only two other blacks: Brigadier General Benjamin O.
Davis, Sr., and his son, Air Force Lieutenant General Benjamin O. Davis, Jr. The elder Davis had retired, leaving
his son as the only black general still on active duty at that
time.

Davison's first thought was of his wife, Jean, who had
supported him without complaint through the long and
difficult struggle up a promotional ladder that sometimes
had seemed to be specially designed for whites. He thought
of her oft-repeated comment, whenever he had confronted
her with a difficult and painful choice. "Do what you have
to do," she always said.

"Does Jean know?" he asked.

"I don't think so," General Edwards replied. "Why don't
you call her?" He picked up his phone and placed a call
to the United States. In moments, Davison was on the line
to Washington, D.C., sharing with his wife the most exciting and rewarding moment in their twenty-eight years of
married life.

Davison, the product of a poverty-stricken boyhood in the District of Columbia ghetto, served in Europe during World War II. He had returned to the United States and was attending Howard University Medical School when he was offered an appointment in the regular army, more than twenty years ago. The young, black medical student did not want to return to the Army, but did so at the urging of the National Association for the Advancement of Colored People.

When the NAACP learned that the appointment had been offered, they urged him to accept it. There was not one black medical officer in the entire Army at the time. If Davison accepted the appointment, the NAACP leaders said, he could apply for medical training in the Army, become the first black medical officer in the service, and open the way for others to follow.

Davison yielded to their urging and, although the discrimination still present in Army policy twenty years ago kept him from achieving the original objective, he still considers himself a living example of what is possible for blacks to achieve within the American political system.

"In my travels I have seen a great deal of other systems," he says. "They leave me convinced that we have the best one here. Sure, you have to keep needling it, but the needling is producing new opportunities as rapidly as blacks prepare themselves to take advantage of them.

"I've spent enough time against a backdrop of discrimination, and within a policy that encouraged it, to be unsympathetic toward the complaints about the way things are now. The progress that has been made to provide opportunities for blacks in the Army is unbelievable."

General Davison was born in Washington on September 20, 1917. His mother and father both were students at Howard University at the time. Fred never knew his father, who died shortly after he was born. His mother, then in her junior year, left college and obtained a job as a receptionist in a doctor's office in order to support herself and the child.

Fred and his mother lived with three of her four brothers and his grandmother in a small three-bedroom house on Q Street, in a neighborhood that was almost totally black. He says he was not aware of discrimination in his early years, because he rarely saw anyone who wasn't of his own race. The three boys maintained the household, with his mother contributing what she could from a salary that never exceeded ninety dollars a month.

When the Depression came, the boy's mother lost her job in the doctor's office, and went to work as a maid. Her wages were so meager that she finally decided to go to New York, where domestics earned a few dollars more. She remained in New York until her death when Fred was nineteen, and the boy was raised by his grandmother. For most of his life he called her "mom."

The grandmother had taught school in Elizabeth City, North Carolina, before she moved to Washington, D.C. She and her father, both slaves, had been sold away from her mother, a heartless practice that was common in slavery days. Eventually he ran away from his owner, taking his daughter with him. He taught himself to read and write, and saw to it that his daughter was educated. Eventually, she married, moved to Washington with her husband, and bore four sons and three daughters. He died while the children were still quite young.

"Grandmother was a remarkably strong person," General Davison recalls. "When grandfather died she decided to raise her family here in Washington, and, by golly, she did. All four of her sons went to college. All but one graduated. One got a doctorate at the University of Illinois and when he retired was associate professor of anatomy at Meharry Medical College. One taught math at a junior high school in the District of Columbia. The third boy worked his way through college as a barber, and then opened his own barber shop. The fourth son got a degree in English—he was a talented writer, quite a poet—but was drowned off Eniwetok in World War II, while trying to save a shipmate from the undertow. The way things were in the Army in those days, he didn't even get a commendation for the hero-ism that cost him his life.

"When I look back on those guys I find it pretty hard to feel sorry for myself, remembering how they dug in. They did every conceivable kind of work—anything they could find for any amount of pay—in order to hold that family together. I could never have done as well myself if it hadn't been for them."

The family circumstances were bleak when Fred was a child, and the house on Q Street was primitive, but he recalls it as one filled with love. His grandmother was firm, but kind, and she held the household together with a strength of character and determination that was an exam-ple for sons and grandson alike.

"You went to school clean, you combed your hair, you took a bath," Davison recalls. "I rarely got hand-me-downs, since I had no older brothers, but the few new clothes I had were expected to last. I recall once getting a new suit and wearing it to play. It got all muddy, and when I re-alized what I had done I tried to wash it off at a water fountain. It didn't work, and when I got home my grand-mother was very angry. She tried to explain the sacrifices my mother was making to get me the things I did have, but all the time she was doing the explaining she was whaling the daylights out of me. I don't know which made the greater impression, the lecture or the beating I took."

"I don't think I regarded myself as poor at the time, but believe me, we were poor," Davison says, wincing a bit as he thinks back to those early days. "My kids won't believe me today when I tell them that I learned to fold cardboard to make a perfect insole to cover the holes in my shoes.

"I remember once, when things were particularly rough, being sent to borrow two dollars from one of my aunts, because there wasn't any food in the house. But we never went hungry. I still marvel at the way my grandmother managed. That same Christmas we were so poor that there wasn't any money for Christmas gifts. I remember, we gave each other things to laugh at. I gave one of my uncles a roll of toilet paper. I guess, in a close family, you can laugh off your troubles, even when things are really rough."

As Fred grew older he enrolled in Sumner-Magruder elementary school. He was a good student, and when he finished there he went on to junior high school and Dunbar High School. He was a member of the National Honor Society when he graduated in 1933.

Fred studied in the kitchen, where he could enjoy the warmth of a coal-burning range. The house had gaslights, but gas was expensive, so he read by the light of a lamp that burned kerosine, which could be had at a nearby store for ten cents a gallon.

When Davison graduated from high school he enrolled in Howard University, where he had won a scholarship that covered his full tuition costs. He attended Howard for six years and never had to pay for anything but books. Money was so scarce, however, that even that was difficult. Often, during the early part of the term, he had to do much of his studying in the library because he had not been able to buy all his books. He took one course in scientific German "without ever getting up enough money to buy the text."

At Howard, Davison had for his adviser a controversial, brilliant professor of zoology, Dr. Hyman Chase. Except for his grandmother, Chase stands out as the major influence in Davison's life.

"Chase was a driver, a perfectionist," Davison says. "He nearly made me climb the walls as my adviser. In my freshman year he told me I didn't need any of the basic courses —I didn't need English, or anything like that—that they had given me all I needed of the basics during indoctrination week. He made me carry a really tough schedule. I had eleven courses in German, six courses in physics, ten semesters of chemistry. During one semester I strayed into a course in philosophy taught by the Rhodes scholar, Alain Locke, and I thought he would die. He always sneered at what he called the 'soft sciences.'

"Chase used to take me to lunch at his apartment. He was a guy who had literally pulled himself up by his own bootstraps, but he had a phenomenal appreciation of good music. The price of my lunch was listening to it. I never did dig opera much, but I learned to like the overtures and symphonies and still do today.

"Going to Chase's classes was a daily battle of wits. He'd ask one question after another, each one getting into something more obscure, until finally you stumbled. He would tolerate no deviation from the total pursuit of scholarship by any of his students."

Davison got his bachelor of science degree from Howard in 1938, with majors in zoology and chemistry. He graduated cum laude, and then continued at Howard to earn his master's degree. While working on the master's in 1940, he and Jean got married. They had been going together since 1935, their freshman year at Howard.

"I bought her the best diamond I could afford," the general recalls. "You could have put it on the head of a pin. When I told Chase I wanted to get married, he said, 'You don't have anything to lose, but I feel sorry for her.'

"When I was in high school I had been on the track team. I ran the quarter mile. One year, without telling Chase, I went out for track at Howard, and things went along all right until we were scheduled to go to the relays at Penn State, and I had to go to him and tell him that I was going to miss class because I would be out of town.

"You would have thought I had told him the world was coming to an end. He ranted and raved at me about taking time from my classes and wasting my life. When I got back he made me take a makeup examination that was worse than a final exam."

Davison remained under the influence of Dr. Chase while in graduate school. The professor drove him unmercifully, but it was for the student's own good, and Fred remembers him with admiration, affection, and gratitude. "He is the person, other than my grandmother, to whom I owe the most in this world," he says.

Davison took one mid-term exam under Chase and knew, when he finished it, that he had written a perfect paper. When he got the examination paper back, it was graded "99." Fred went to the teacher and pointed out that there wasn't a mark on the paper, so why had he received a "99"?

"I never give a student '100,'" Chase replied. "If I did you would think you were good."

While in graduate school Davison worked from 11:30 at night until 7:00 in the morning, and also worked during the day as an assistant in the laboratory. He went to sleep while on duty in the laboratory early one evening and Dr. Chase discovered him, nodding in the chair. The professor gave his prize student an unmerciful tongue-lashing, pointing out that much of their equipment was irreplaceable, and if he slept he might fall over and break some priceless item. There was no money to buy another.

"I don't really know when I was sleeping those days," Davison says. "Just catch-as-catch-can, I guess, and I was awfully tired. I thought Chase was being awfully unreasonable, and it rubbed me the wrong way. I got mad—furious —and sulked for a couple of days.

"Finally he came to me and said, 'You can sulk if you want to, but just remember, I can forget you a lot easier than you can forget me.' I've thought of that comment often in later years, in other situations. It was a useful lesson for me."

While at Howard, Fred was in ROTC. When he graduated he joined the 428th Reserve Regiment, an all-black
infantry outfit made up mostly of men from ROTC, almost
all of whom had college degrees.

"The regiment was held together by the will of the commanding officer, West Hamilton, who had been one of the
rare Negro officers in World War I," Davison says. "He is
responsible more than any other man for the blacks in the
Army who have reached the grade of colonel."

Davison received his M.S. degree, cum laude, in 1940,
and soon thereafter the 428th was ordered to active duty.
Fred was in a portion of the unit that was activated as the
366th Infantry Regiment, which must have been one of
the most highly educated outfits in the armed forces. Of
120-odd officers, all black, there were only three who did
not hold college degrees.

The regiment went first to Fort Devens, Massachusetts,
where Davison's and Chase's paths crossed again. Chase
was assigned as operations officer of the regiment. They were
trans-shipped to Africa and sent on to Italy. In December,
1944, the 366th was deactivated, and Davison, now a captain, was reassigned to the 371st Infantry Regiment.

Davison went to France as the commander of a light
infantry company where he had his first serious brush with
military authority. One of his friends, a major in another
battalion, was having a feud with his regimental commander.

"The commander had the officer restricted," Davison
recalls. "There was a good bit of pressure on the other officers to keep him in isolation. I wasn't in his battalion, but
I visited him and took him things that he needed. Finally,
the regimental commander called me in and questioned
me, suggesting that I was being disloyal to him because
of my relationship with my friend. I told him that, if all
of his officers were as loyal to him as I was to my friends,
he was a lucky man.

"I fell from favor because of that, but, you know, somewhere along the line you pick up a code. You never forget a debt you owe to another person, and I knew that I could never repay the debt I owed to my friend."

Davison's company had been in the front lines for several months when it was deactivated at the end of the war. He applied for appointment in the regular army, but his request was denied, and he was separated from the service in 1946. He returned to Washington and enrolled in medical school at Howard University under the GI Bill. It was at the end of his first year of medical school that he was offered an appointment in the regular army, accepted it at the urging of the NAACP, and on July 1, 1947, reported for duty as a first lieutenant at Fort Dix.

Soon after his arrival at the New Jersey base Davison filed his application for medical training. Months passed and he received no response. He filed a second application and this one, too, was ignored. Meanwhile, he was assigned to training duty with a new ROTC training unit that was being organized at A&M College in Orangeburg, South Carolina.

In mid-August of 1948, with the school year approaching, Davison went to Washington to find out what had happened to his application for medical school. The Chief of Infantry Branch looked at him across his desk and said coldly that he would not approve his application because if he did Davison would continue to acquire seniority at the expense of his fellow officers. Besides, he said, there was no assurance that Davison would succeed in medical school.

Davison pointed out that he had already earned two degrees, cum laude, and successfully completed a year of medical school, but it was to no avail. The officer told him that if he insisted on becoming a doctor he had two choices: he could apply for leave without pay, or he could resign.

"There was little doubt that my request was denied because I was black," Davison says. "But I guess I resented his manner more than his words. There was a complete lack of the slightest amenities. As a general I wouldn't stand a private in front of me and talk to him the way he talked to me as a captain when he was a colonel. But, in retrospect, he was just part of the times, and there may be some justice in the fact that he was still a colonel when he retired."

Davison left the office and went to the Howard University campus, where he talked with the dean of the medical school. He was told that if he tried to return to school after a two-year lapse he would have to begin anew. The first of their four daughters had already been born, and Davison decided to remain in the Army.

During his three years with the ROTC unit at A&M Davison had been promoted to captain, and in September 1950, he was sent to Fort Benning, Georgia, to enroll in the Student Advanced Infantry Officer Course. He remained there until April, 1951, and was promoted to major during that time.

During the final months of the course the class knew that it was going to be sent to Korea, but, five days before they were scheduled to leave, Davison and twenty-nine others were called out and told that they were going to Turkey to be assigned to the mission there. The major had all of his shots and was on leave, preparing to leave for Turkey, when he got a call from the Pentagon.

"They said they had a special assignment for me in Germany," he recalls. "It was very, very special. It was so special that when I reported in overseas they didn't even know I was coming. I realized then that apparently it had suddenly dawned on someone that they had one black guy in the unit that was going to Turkey, and that this could never be."

After some delay in deciding what to do with him, Davison was assigned to the 370th Armored Infantry Battalion at Munich, and spent three years there. He says that "getting pulled out of the Turkey detail was then and still is annoying, but at Munich I had the opportunity to really put in practice what I had learned in the Advanced Course, and professionally those were the three most productive years I have ever spent."

"You can get an awful lot out of wherever you are placed if you put enough into it," he says.

While in Munich Davison had what he calls "another instance of having to face up to reality." He was operations officer of the battalion, and one day arrived at his office to find a sergeant waiting outside the door. The man was not in his unit, but he knew him and knew that he was a good sergeant who performed his duties well.

"He asked if he could talk to me and I told him to come in," Davison recalls. "He told me he was in trouble and asked me if I would defend him in a court-martial that was coming up. I told him I would investigate the case and let him know.

"The charges were being supported by the battalion commander, who, to put it kindly, was an unperceptive man. I checked into the charges and found that, while what the sergeant had done was wrong, it would have been condoned as common practice if it had been done by anyone else. I was convinced that the court-martial was founded on prejudice, and although it meant fighting my battalion commander, I decided to take the case. I knew the hazards of doing so, and explained them to Jean, but after she gave me her usual 'do what you have to do,' I knew I had no choice.

"There were three charges against the sergeant, and several specifications on each charge. He was acquitted of all but one specification on one of the charges, and for that he got a tap on the wrist. I later discovered that the battalion commander whom I had opposed took his revenge through a subtle comment in my efficiency report: 'This officer sometimes imagines prejudice where none exists.' It delayed my attendance at War College by at least two years."

Nevertheless, Davison did better than the officer who tried to do him in. The battalion commander, not long after that, was relieved of his command. He ultimately was promoted to colonel, but by that time Davison was in the career branch in the Pentagon, and the officer got his promotion only after coming to him and begging for help.

"He was a weakling," Davison says, "and I look back on him with contempt."

After three years in Germany, Davison returned to the United States in September of 1954 to attend the Command and General Staff School at Fort Leavenworth, Kansas. When he completed the course in July, 1955, he was assigned to the Pentagon for a four-year hitch in the infantry branch.

"There, for the first time, I worked with people who were all top grade," Davison says. "I was in tough competition with people who didn't have to hide behind the color of their skin in order to gain an advantage. Infantry branch people really measured you in terms of what you could produce. They didn't care whether you were black, blue, green, or yellow as long as you could do the job.

"Once you get in that whirlpool you go on to better jobs, and the circle gets tighter and tighter. I was sent to Korea in 1959 and 1960 in the personnel services division of the Eighth Army. Then I came back to Second Army Headquarters at Fort Meade. I stayed there until 1962 when I was sent to War College at Carlisle Barracks. The circle was getting tighter now, and I was really working with top people.

"In 1963 I came back to the Pentagon to work in the office of the Under Secretary of the Army, and stayed there until 1965. I worked for Arthur W. Allen, Deputy Under

Ernie Banks: He shared poverty with five brothers and seven sisters. His recollections of his Dallas childhood show no bitterness or regret. They were not aware that they were deprived.

Jesse Jackson: This fiery preacher sees himself as a catalyst of black economic power, which he regards as "the most powerful weapon of the black to gain a fair share of the nation's affluence."

Richard Hatcher: Mayor Hatcher's salary is less than he made in private law practice. A bachelor, he says he has a big family to worry about—the children of Gary, Indiana.

James Brown: Even in America, long hailed as the land of oppor—
tunity, grade school dropout, ex-con James Brown's meteoric rise
from rags to riches is almost too much to believe.

Anna Langford: "Young people must not be discouraged because they are living in
a deprived environment. They must tell themselves, as I did, to do something about
getting themselves out of it."

Shirley Chisholm: The congresswoman says, "I know there are homes where there isn't enough to eat . . . but if children are to escape, they must first have an education."

Frederic E. Davison: This brigadier general in the Army of the U.S., above with Secretary of Defense Melvin R. Laird, believes there is no substitute for proving you can do as much as anyone else, black or white.

James Tilmon: When he was a kid he decided to become a pilot. He didn't know then there were no black pilots. When he made that startling discovery he resolved to be the first and he was.

M. Earl Grant: His savings and loan institution has assets of more than $33 million. He used to be chef-cook on a railroad dining car.

Manford Byrd: That Byrd should rise to the most responsible and demanding post in public education held by a black man in America is something of a paradox. His father was sixty-three before he learned to read and write.

Gwendolyn Brooks: Pulitzer Prize winner for poetry. "I think the most exciting part of my life is right now, not because of my literary work but because of what I do with young people."

John Shepherd: Says this entrepreneur, "We must think of ourselves as Americans first and black second."

John H. Johnson: Head of *Ebony, Negro Digest, Jet,* and *Tan*—combined circulation 3 million copies a month. He says, "If [a black] makes something of himself he also contributes favorably to the total image of black people."

James Farmer: "What black people really want and need is not very complex. . . . The most important thing for us is to be accepted as human beings . . . we'll make it the rest of the way by ourselves."

Secretary for Manpower and Reserve Forces. He was a man who really knew staff work—very demanding—and I would say that he was the man in the recent past who gave me the most help."

In November, 1965, Davison was assigned to Fort Bliss, Texas, as commanding officer of the Third Training Brigade. He worked there for two years, and then volunteered for duty in Vietnam.

"Jean and the children couldn't understand it, and still don't. It caused real trauma in our household when I told them I was going to volunteer, but Jean said, as always, 'Do what you have to do.' And it *was* something I *had* to do.

"We were getting some fine young black officers at that time, and they really watched me, a senior citizen. I kept telling them to go to Vietnam—that Vietnam was where the action was and it would really help their careers. But it kept getting harder and harder to tell them to go when I did not go myself. Besides, I really felt, deep down, that I ought to be where the action was."

Davison was assigned to the 199th Light Infantry Brigade in November, 1967, as deputy brigade commander. He was acting commander when "the VC obliged with the Tet offensive, and it wasn't difficult to chew them up. We had good people in the brigade, and it was simply a matter of using their talents and skills. Bingo. The brigadier-general list came out and I was on it. It was the realization of what had many times seemed an impossible dream."

Davison returned to the Pentagon in May of 1969 as Director of Enlisted Personnel. He now lives comfortably with his wife and younger children in a pleasant home on Washington's northwest side, and his old friend, Dr. Hyman Chase, lives nearby. Chase, who has retired from the Army, is in his third career as an assistant professor of anatomy in Howard's College of Medicine. Mrs. Davison teaches in the District of Columbia schools and also has an active life working with a number of projects devoted to furthering the progress of her race.

Davison is convinced that most of the discrimination that remains in the Army stems from "individual ignorance and stupidity," and that the situation for blacks is improving all the time.

"I recall working in the infantry branch with a long, lean Texan," he says. "He was a fine guy—a straight guy—and I had worked with him for a long time. One day we were in the office and he was talking on the phone. I think it was right after the election in 1956, and he was arguing with the guy at the other end of the line. The argument got more heated and finally I heard him say, 'You talk just like a West Texas nigger.'

"A dead silence followed. When I looked over at him after a moment he was sitting there with his neck and face as red as a beet. Finally he hung up the phone, came over to me, and said, 'Fred, I'm sorry. I just don't know what to say.'

"I told him to forget it; that what he had said didn't bother me because he had told me by his behavior as long as I had known him how he really felt about things. And it didn't bother me, but if I hadn't known him so well I would have written him off. I think that sort of thing often happens, because of the way attitudes have been in our country for so many years."

Davison says you see those same attitudes reflected in the differences in human behavior between men in combat and those who are not on the firing line.

"When men are together in the fire zones, nobody cares whether the guy next to him is black or white," Davison says. "You only care whether he is a man, and whether you can rely on him when the going gets tough. But when you get back to the main base, or in town on a pass, people tend to seek out other people with whom they are comfortable, and superficial things again become important to them. I think there is also a tendency on the part of some white soldiers to behave artificially because of what society —in a country that has practiced intolerance for so long —may think of them if they associate with blacks.

"But in spite of those differences between attitudes in combat and attitudes outside, I am convinced that, once a man has learned those lessons in the harsh realities of combat, they are never really forgotten. They may be submerged, but they are not forgotten.

"I have talked with the investigating teams that have gone to some of the bases where racial incidents have occurred. They tell me that, more often than not, the men who were in combat in Vietnam have either not been involved, or have involved themselves by actively coming to the assistance of men of the other race. Because of their experience they were able to transcend the racial thing.

"It made me feel good to discover this. Obviously, nothing can ever really make anyone feel good about the casualties we have had to take in Vietnam. But if the experience of tens of thousands of youngsters over there created in them a willingness to try to understand those of different races and nationalities and creeds, then I damn near think Vietnam was worth it. Those who died will not have died in vain because they have helped to contribute to understanding, and we desperately need understanding in this country."

"Loyalty and real friendship don't know any color," says Davison. "Along the way you get help from all kinds of people, some black and some white. Nobody ever gets anywhere without getting help from others along the line. I think in my case the early help came from other blacks, and in the later years most of the help came from others who were white."

Davison says that, to achieve success, he doesn't know any substitute for working and proving that you can do as much as anyone else. He tells his own children that if they are able, have intelligence, and are willing to work they can do almost anything they want to do.

"Don't expect anyone to give you anything," he says. "Maybe, if you are black, you have to do 205 percent in order to get credit for 100 percent for what you did, but remember, if you do work that hard you will have 105 percent more knowledge and ability than the other guy, and nobody can take that away from you.

"We all know that blacks have not had the opportunities that were available to whites in the past, but it is silly to think we can overcome that by trying to create a viable, separate black community. It is just pipe dreaming, and it can't be done. Even if it were possible, America couldn't afford it. This country is pressed enough as it is to retain its preeminence, without being divided within itself.

"Someone has to force doors open but that doesn't mean crashing them down. And once the doors are opened there must be people who are prepared to walk through them, to take advantage of the opportunities they will find inside.

"That's the real challenge to the young blacks of this country—to get themselves prepared for the opportunities that lie behind that open door."

8

M. Earl Grant

Black Capitalist

M. Earl Grant's life has been guided by a number of maxims, most of which he coined himself. One of his favorites
is: You don't get paid for *having* brains; you get paid for
using them. It is an apothegm that he has applied often
during a life that had its roots in poverty on a West Virginia farm, and flowered into affluence under the Southern
California sun.

One of Grant's early opportunities to apply that principle
came in 1916, when he was working as a chef-cook on a
Rock Island Railroad dining car. The decision that resulted
changed the course of his life.

Grant was in his kitchen, cleaning up after a run, when
a messenger came to him and asked that he report to the
superintendent's office. The cook finished his work quickly
and went to the office, where he found his boss and a
strange man waiting for him. He was told that the stranger
was going to be the new steward on his dining car.

"I sat there in a big, deep leather chair, smoking an expensive cigar that the super had given me, while he showed
the new steward a stack of compliments two feet high,"
Grant recalls. "They had come from passengers on my dining car bragging on the service and the food. Then he went

119

on and explained to the man what the steward's job was all about.

" 'Grant is a chef-cook,' he said. 'He's one of my best men. He can do anything in that dining car. He'll do everything else, and if you can make change you can make good as a steward.'

"There was a little more conversation and a few minutes later I walked out of that office as proud as a peacock. I went over to State Street to catch a trolley car, thinking about all the compliments the superintendent had paid me. While I was standing there waiting for the trolley I must have started *using* my brains, because all of a sudden I realized the significance of what the superintendent had said.

"What he had really told me was that he knew I was capable of being the new steward, but I wasn't going to get the job because I was black. To add injury to insult, I would have to train the white man for a job that should have been mine, and they were going to pay him an extra sixty dollars a month. I could do his work for him, but I could never aspire to his job.

"Right in that instant, the Rock Island Railroad lost the best chef-cook it had ever had. I realized I had gone as far in life as I would ever go if I stayed in that job."

Grant quit his job a few days later and went to California. The railroad lost a chef, but California gained a new black citizen who ultimately would become a millionaire. Today, as chairman of the board of the Family Savings and Loan Association, Grant presides over an institution with assets of more than $33 million. He founded it when a white banker refused to loan him money to buy a house, and he now personally controls more than half of the stock.

The black financier is a robust man who stands over six feet tall and weighs 235 pounds. He looks at least twenty years younger than his seventy-eight years. Although his hair is thinning and turning gray, his face is full, his skin firm, and he speaks with a strong, resonant voice. He is rich not only in money, but also in wit and wisdom, and, although his attitude has mellowed since the days when he settled arguments with his fists, he remains a young militant in spite of his years.

Today, sitting in his comfortable office in a half-million-dollar building designed for him by the famed black architect, Paul R. Williams, he recalls his own experience as he cites his philosophy for others who want to get ahead.

"Do what you can do," he says. "Shine shoes, if necessary, or pick up rubbish and garbage like I did, but don't stay there all your life. Keep your eyes open and be alert for something better that you can do next."

"I've been working ever since I was big enough to work," Grant says, with a twinkle in his eyes. "I was born on a farm at four o'clock in the afternoon, and my mother made me pick up some chips to cook supper with that night."

Grant smiles at his exaggeration, but it isn't too many years away from the truth. He was born on a farm owned by a man named Shattuck. The farm, located along the Ohio River near Parkersburg, West Virginia, encompassed several hundred acres and was worked by Grant's family with two other families he describes as "the tobacco-road type."

The entire family was hired out to the owner, so when they were old enough, all thirteen Grant children worked. So did their mother, who milked thirteen cows every morning, and again every night. The pay, for all fifteen, was a dollar a day.

Eventually, Grant's father and grandfather had the opportunity to buy an adjoining piece of land. They divided it, and his father kept the part that contained the house.

"It was a pretty decent house," Grant recalls. "It had an atticlike upstairs that had four rooms in it. The children slept there, and mother and father slept in another bedroom downstairs. The only heat was in the kitchen and in one fireplace. We burned coal because it was cheaper than going out and chopping wood. I can still remember when coal went up to three cents a bushel. That was a terrible price."

Grant says he didn't really feel that his family was poor because so many other families who didn't have their own land were worse off than they.

"The farm was between two main roads," he says, "and quite often people would walk across to take a shortcut from one road to the other. It always made me feel pretty proud that they were walking on our ground."

The family was never hungry, because there was plenty of food on the farm. They not only raised enough vegetables and hogs to feed themselves, but had enough left over to sell in town to pay the taxes and buy needed supplies and clothing. Grant's grandfather developed a produce route, and his grandmother drove the wagon, stopping at each house while the grandson jumped off and made deliveries in a basket to the back door. In summer they put food by for the winter, and Grant says he still knows "how to preserve, to can, and to dry."

"The doctor came to my house just one time while I was growing up," Grant recalls. "That was when my grandmother fell off the wagon and broke her arm. Mother and grandmother were of the old school that knew better where to find medicine in the woods than the doctor did. They had remedies for everything, and grandmother was a midwife although she had no training and couldn't even read or write.

"Although I never felt we were poor, when I look back on those days, it is clear that we certainly were. We rarely had spending money as kids, and a nickel looked as big as a wagon wheel. We'd buy shoes in the fall of the year and take them off when summer came to save them until it got cold again. There were times when only half of us could go to Sunday school, and the other half had to stay home because there weren't enough clothes to go around. If I had a pair of pants and my brother a shirt, I'd have to borrow his shirt or he had to borrow my pants, and the other one stayed home. Not being able to go to church was always a terrible disappointment, because we had nothing like TV or radio in those days, and the big excitement of the week was to go to Sunday school."

Grant still remembers the names of his first and second grade teachers because that's as far in school as he managed to get.

"You get educated by more than books if you live as long as I have," he says, "but a formal education is a lot more necessary today. Even when I was younger I was always at a disadvantage and had to fight that much harder because I didn't have that book learning.

"Mother and father were willing to have us get an education, but a man who has a houseful of kids and has never done anything but farm doesn't know where to turn. My father had never been to school although he learned to read small letters, but my mother could read and write. Because of all the discrimination there was, even against the best-educated Negroes, they couldn't see much advantage in getting an education, other than learning to read and write."

Grant was twelve years old when he registered for the third grade, but he soon had to drop out. He was big enough to help with the major farm chores, and his help was needed because the family lived off the land, and workers were needed if they were to survive. The younger members of the family fared better, because they were able to get an education with the help of the older children who by then were able to work.

As a youngster, Grant resented deeply the discriminatory practices to which he was exposed, and that resentment was to stay with him, and motivate him, for the rest of his life. There was one school for blacks in Parkersburg and all the others were restricted to whites. The boy had to walk past half a dozen of them in order to get to the black school, which had all the grades in one building. Sometimes he had to fight all the way there and all the way back.

"I guess my worst experience with prejudice was one I had when I was eight," Grant recalls. "I'll never forget it if I live to be a hundred like my mother or as old as my grandmother who died when she was 105.

"We had a neighbor lady who was very poor. She had only a small piece of land that her father had left her, with enough room for a small garden, and that was all. She really lived off the land, and one day she asked me to go picking blackberries with her in a nearby pasture, because she was afraid the bull or the cows might get after her.

"We were picking berries when these two white ladies came along, and the three women fussed at each other a little bit. I guess they resented her picking berries there. I didn't think anything about it, but one day about two weeks later my father told me that I had to go into town with him.

"When we got to town we went into the courthouse, and I was taken in front of the justice of the peace. They accused me of helping the neighbor lady attack the two white women we had met in the field.

"Of course, I hadn't attacked anybody. I was nothing but a little kid with a tin bucket in my hand picking blackberries. But they told me to plead guilty anyway. So I told the justice that I hadn't done anything, but that I had been told to plead guilty. He dropped the hammer on me and said, 'Eight dollars fine.'

"That shook me up and I carried it with me for a long time because it was so unjust and unfair. My father made only a dollar a day, and eight dollars was a fortune to him. But they could fine me eight dollars because they were in power and I was not. The judge must have known I wasn't guilty, because what could an eight-year-old boy do to two grown women who weighed 180 pounds apiece, out in a berry field?"

Three of Grant's grandparents were slaves who had not learned to read or write when they were young because of Virginia laws that prohibited the education of slaves. His grandfather used to tell him of the earlier days when many Virginia plantation owners had run huge slave-breeding farms, and made fortunes shipping black slaves farther south. The stories his grandfather told, coupled with the discrimination he experienced himself, embittered but did not discourage him.

"I realized when I was in my teens that no one was going to come along and make life pleasant for me," he says. "I knew I was going to have to do something about it myself. It wouldn't do any good to just sit around belly-aching about what they did to my grandparents—I had to start worrying about what their grandson did for himself.

"I can understand how some of the kids feel today, because bitter experiences become indelible in your mind. You resent the insults that you take and long for revenge. But I've learned over the years that nothing is really accomplished by reacting violently. Besides, all people, no matter what color they are, are not as ornery as some of the people. If you try, there is always somebody who is willing to come and help you."

When Grant was sixteen he went to Parkersburg, where he got a job making deliveries for a shoe store. He didn't have a bicycle and couldn't afford to buy one, so he walked from one end of town to the other. In wet weather orders for rubbers would pour into the store. The youngster sloshed through the rain in sodden sneakers, delivering rubbers to others although he had none of his own.

After working in the shoe store for about a year, he realized that he would never get ahead unless he accumulated some money. He was earning only three-and-one-half dollars a week, most of which went to pay for his room and board, but whenever he could he saved a dollar and put it in the bank.

His thrift paid off in an unexpected way when the banker's wife, observing his efforts to make something of himself, offered him a job which provided his room and board and five dollars a week. He worked for her for about a year, finally saving enough money to enable him to go to Pittsburgh, the nearest big city, which was about 140 miles away.

After trying in countless other places, Grant at last got a job working for the Pennsylvania Railroad, washing dishes on a dining car. One day the steward "talked down" to him and called him an insulting name, and Grant—a husky young man who weighed two hundred pounds and was over six feet tall—expressed his resentment with his fists. The steward learned a lesson but so did Grant. He lost the job it had taken him so long to get.

Instead of looking for another job in Pittsburgh, Grant went to Chicago. He worked briefly for the Illinois Central Railroad, and then got a job washing dishes for the Rock Island, where he also learned to cook.

"I was making progress," Grant recalls, "but I still thought I could settle everything with my fists. My name was at the top of the list for a job as chief on a new California run, but then I got in a fight with an inspector. Because I had lost my temper I also lost the job as second cook. It cost me $50 a month for the next three years, just to have had an instant's pleasure calling that man a liar. That was when I started thinking like a mature man. I wasn't but twenty-two then, but I realized that it was too costly to me to have the satisfaction of cussing a man out and running off at the mouth. That's when I learned that if you are going to live and get ahead in this world you have to get along with people."

Grant finally became the youngest chef-cook on the Rock

Island Railroad, and the best one, and it was then that he realized that he could go no further and quit his job to go to California. He left the railroad without expressing any displeasure over his experience, following another of his maxims, "Even when you don't like a job, you should never make anyone mad or get fired, because the time might come when you'll be glad to go back there."

Realizing that as long as he wore a jacket and apron he'd remain a servant, Grant traded them for some overalls when he got to California. He decided that if he worked eighteen hours a day he could achieve some measure of independence. Grant's size played a huge role in his decision to go into the rubbish business. Weighing 260 pounds, he felt "too fat" and "wanted to work some of it off."

Grant found an unincorporated area that didn't have any rubbish collection, bought a truck for $160, and just before Christmas in 1923 started looking for customers. He firmly resolved that he would always have a pleasant "good morning" for his customers no matter what their attitude was. He charged them twenty dollars a month and his business flourished. It wasn't very long before his income skyrocketed to six thousand dollars a month.

It was time to expand. Grant decided to bid on some garbage contracts in the Los Angeles suburbs. The city manager in Pasadena, an old acquaintance, suggested that he bid on the garbage contract there. Grant went to the sanitation department but was refused a bid sheet. The city manager intervened and Grant submitted his bid, but the department would not accept it. The entrepreneur again related his difficulties to the city manager, and his friend phoned the city engineer to request an explanation.

"That guy's a rich nigger," was the reply.

"I know he is," the city manager said, "but that rich nigger is sitting right here at my desk and I'll back his bid."

Although he lost out on that contract, Grant subsequently

obtained others to collect the garbage in Burbank and Alta-
dena, but the resolution of one problem soon created another. Where could he dispose of the additional trash?
Grant recalled that back home in West Virginia his father
had picked up garbage from other families to feed his
hogs. Grant's garbage soon turned to silver when he began selling it to ranchers who raised pigs near Los Angeles.

Grant's trucks hadn't been rolling to the hog farms for
very long before he concluded that it didn't make much
sense for him to let other people's hogs grow fat on his
garbage. After a bit of searching he found a piece of land
that he could buy for fifteen hundred dollars. He invested
an additional $325 in six sows, a boar, and nineteen pigs,
and now had a hog farm of his own.

"When I started out on that farm I still thought the garbage collection business was the dog and the hog business
was the dog's tail," he says. "But after three years I discovered that the tail was wagging the dog."

Grant launched his hog farm in 1928, just before the Depression, which was disastrous timing for many new enterprises of that era, but the hog business prospered in
spite of the hard times.

"Fur coats get exchanged for pork chops when people
get hungry," he philosophizes.

Apparently a lot of fur coats got exchanged for Grant's
pork chops, because he soon became one of the largest hog
feeders in California. When the enterprise reached its peak,
the ambitious rancher was feeding garbage to six thousand
pigs, and sometimes sold as many as ten thousand dollars'
worth of hogs in a single day.

The secret of his phenomenal success, he says, was the
quality of the hogs he produced. Through skillful breeding
Grant produced hogs which brought as much as ten dollars
a head more than those of other ranchers.

"If you pick a boar for good qualities you can't go wrong
because eighty percent of the pigs take after their fathers,"

he says. "I always tried to produce an ideal hog with good hams, a wide back for pork chops, and deep sides for bacon."

His success attracted the attention of the California Hog Feeders' Association, an all-white group, and he was invited to join the organization. Eventually he became a member of the board of directors.

The hog business ultimately began making so many demands on his time that he turned the rubbish business over to a brother. During World War II, when help was scarce, he devoted his full time to pitching thirty tons of garbage a day. When Grant disposed of the ranch in 1952, in order to concentrate on a less strenuous career, his original fifteen-hundred-dollar investment brought a return of three hundred thousand dollars.

Perhaps that is why he says, "The smell of garbage never bothered me. It was a sweet smell—the sweetest smell in the world to me."

When Grant began to make more money than he needed to support himself, his wife Flora, and his son Don, and to expand his other enterprises, he began to buy rundown properties and rehabilitate them to increase their value. One day in 1947, driving by the African Methodist Episcopal Church in Pasadena, he saw a "For Sale" sign on a home right across the street from the church.

It looked like an attractive property to be repaired and resold so he made a deposit on it, but when he went to a white-owned bank to secure a loan they refused to grant it. They said that the white neighbors would object, and that if they made a loan to him it would get them in trouble with the real estate brokers.

Grant has never allowed the word "No" to discourage him, so he concluded that if the white banks wouldn't give him a mortgage, he would start a lending institution of his own. He became one of the organizers of the Broadway Federal Savings and Loan Association of Los Angeles, which today is the largest black-owned savings and loan association in America.

Two years later Grant founded the Watts Savings and Loan Association. The total capital stock and paid-in surplus of that association originally was $165,000. Within six months, working without pay, Grant built the assets to $430,000, and a year later they had grown to $1,500,000. Only at the end of the first year did he begin paying himself a salary of fifty dollars a month. Today the assets of the association, now renamed Family Savings, are $33 million.

During the Watts riots virtually every building in the block was burned except Watts Savings and Loan. The institution lost eight hundred thousand in deposits over a weekend. Yet Grant acknowledges that the militance of recent years, coupled with the warnings contained in the Kerner report, have increased the business of the firm. A hundred big businesses are now depositors in his savings and loan that he "never could get a quarter out of before."

Grant says he favors "black power" if it is the kind that is really "green power," that seeks to develop the economic strength of the black community.

"If you drive out of your way to come to my little gasoline station and help me to make money so I can educate my children you're doing something about black power," he says. "Negroes have got to go out of their way to help each other.

"What do we produce which would help us survive if the other group, with all its know-how, went out the window? In the State of California we don't produce enough wheat to make a loaf of bread. And the younger generation wouldn't know how to cook it."

Yet Grant is not one of the senior citizens who are unsympathetic with today's generation. He says that "as a youngster I thought I could settle things with my fists, so I'd probably be in there swinging with some of these youngsters now." He is disturbed, however, by the anger he sees in some of today's young black people.

"When you're angry, you can't think straight," he says. "When a person is angry, he is partially demented. To be mad at half the people you see on the street is frustrating. That doesn't mean I'm a softy. If you back me into a corner, I will give you a hell of a fight."

The black financier says he feels that in the years ahead business and government, working together, will bring about improvements in the lot of the nation's black and poor. He says the laws are there, but in the past the desire has not been there, and the social institutions that should have been concerned about social problems have failed to try to solve them.

"The churches have missed the boat," the outspoken capitalist says. "They have been taking advantage of emotions while they were living high on the hog."

But Grant says blacks "will have to apply themselves as individuals, because government and business will have to start with individuals; they can't just exercise some magic to improve the condition of an entire group.

"Every black youngster who wants to make something of himself should look in the mirror and realize that if anything good is going to happen to him he is the one that has to make it happen.

"Some people are born great. Some attain greatness. But too many are satisfied just to feel great. You won't get anywhere in this world waiting for something good to happen to you."

9

Shirley Chisholm

Tempest on Capitol Hill

Congresswoman Shirley Chisholm's constituents in the poverty-stricken Bedford-Stuyvesant section of Brooklyn, New York, regard her as a ray of hope in a Congress they feel has given too low a priority to their pressing needs. Not so the entrenched, aging, conservative leaders in the House of Representatives. They take a less sanguine view of the tempestuous lady politician—the first woman of her race to serve in Congress—regarding her as a black plague that threatens some of their most cherished prerogatives.

In the tradition-bound halls of Congress, it is the rule that freshman members shall be seen and not heard until they have been indoctrinated with all of that body's crusty rules and formalities. These require, among other things, that an adversary be addressed as "my good friend and colleague, the distinguished gentleman from so-and-so," before you spit in his face. Mrs. Chisholm made it clear, almost from the moment she took her place in the marble chamber of the House, that respectful silence was not to be one of her endearing virtues. She lost no time disavowing any intention of being seen and not heard.

"They're going to hear from *me*," she announced to the newsmen who keep watch on Capitol Hill. "Congress is badly in need of reform and I'm going to fight for this. We must change our priorities."

Then, uncorking a bare-knuckled blow at the power structure in the House of Representatives, she added:

"It is shocking to me that there are so many old men with such power over the destiny of the country who are so much out of touch, out of tune, with the country. It's just shocking. Maybe I was expecting too much. The seniority system is horrible. The experience of people is important, but in a dynamic country like this, it is not right to reward people just for length of service.

"People have to have creativity and fresh outlooks about problems. The thing that happens to a lot of old men is that they are not attuned to what's happening. There must be a way to make more use of younger members with capacity and talent to help lead this country. We must open the doors of leadership to congressmen and congresswomen with something more to give than mere longevity of service. Men of experience are necessary, but so are men of real ability.

"We are in bad shape in this country, and I believe one of the reasons is that we are running the country by traditional rules that are obsolescent for today's needs."

The occasion for Mrs. Chisholm's maiden outburst was the announcement of the House leadership that she had been assigned a seat on the Agriculture committee. Since any farming done in her congested urban district would have to take place on a forty-foot lot, she regarded the assignment at best as an affront and at worst as an attempt to isolate her on a committee with the least possible relevance to her interests and her constituency—a vineyard in which her militance would have little chance to flower.

"Apparently all they know here in Washington about Brooklyn is that a tree grew there," the black congresswoman said. "I can think of no other reason for assigning me to the House Agriculture committee."

Mrs. Chisholm, a slightly built 105-pound bundle of energy, characterizes herself as "a firm, tough woman," and she proved it in her initial encounter. She challenged the House leadership before the Democratic caucus and won. They took her off the committee on Agriculture and put her on the Veterans committee. She would have preferred Education and Labor, but at least her present assignment has relevance to the concerns of many people in her district, and in forcing the change she had made her point.

Victims of Mrs. Chisholm's wrath seeking to place the blame for her unrelenting and sometimes abrasive determination can look to her imposing, six-foot-three-inch grandmother, who raised Shirley when she was a small child. Although she and her three sisters were born in Brooklyn, their parents took them to Barbados when Shirley was three, and they lived there with their grandmother until the child was ten years old.

Her parents returned to the United States with the objective of working as hard as they could and saving money that would enable them to give their children "a very good education."

"This was always uppermost in the minds of my parents," Mrs. Chisholm says. "Since they did not have a formal education they felt it was very important, that education was the key to everything. They vowed that if nothing else they were going to give their daughters a good education. My mother would put by even two or three cents at a time against the day we would enroll in college. In the end, however, three of us got scholarships and paid our own way, and my parents were able to take the money they had saved and buy a house."

Shirley's grandmother was a very stern and demanding woman who imposed the strictest discipline on the children, and early taught them a sense of responsibility to themselves and to others.

"She gave me the philosophy that made me a strong woman," Mrs. Chisholm says. "She always used to say you must have courage and conviction and remember that, when you take a stand on things in this world, quite often you are going to find yourself alone. How often I have found that true in my own political experience. There have been so many times when I have had to stand alone, but I have the guts and the courage to do it because of what this wonderful old lady did for me as a child. She imprinted on my mind the necessity to fight for that in which you believe, even though you may not always have supporters."

Mrs. Chisholm is extremely grateful for the education she received in Barbados. She was reading at three and writing by the time she was four. She had a near-genius IQ, and when she returned to school in America she was well ahead of her peers, a circumstance which she attributes to the superior quality of instruction in the British school system.

"They had a more serious approach to education on the part of both children and teachers," she says. "They were more strict, permitted less freedom, and the result was better preparation of the student."

Shirley and her family lived for a time in the Brownsville area of Brooklyn and then moved to a home on Ralph Avenue in Bedford-Stuyvesant. At that time Brownsville was an integrated, primarily Jewish neighborhood, but Bedford-Stuyvesant was already predominantly black.

The family was very poor. Shirley's parents both worked when they could, her mother as a seamstress, and her father as an unskilled laborer in a burlap bag factory, where he sorted and packaged bags. Although Shirley was only eleven, her parents left her each day with a latchkey around her neck to care for her younger sisters. She took the younger girls to school in the morning, brought them home, and prepared their lunch, "and made sure that they ate it." The child was given a dime a week for her allowance, but didn't always get it because sometimes her parents just didn't have ten cents that they could spare.

"At one time during the Depression we were on welfare," Mrs. Chisholm recalls. "We would get an allotment of clothing each month. Mother always had trouble with me because I was so proud I refused to wear the welfare dresses to school. They were so obviously welfare that some of the other children would jeer. Sometimes mother had to whip me to get me to put on the dress and go to school."

Even in their darkest days, Mrs. Chisholm does not recall food as having been a problem. "Mother was a good cook," she says. "She could pick up the most unappetizing things and make a tasty meal of them, so that even though we were poor we never really did have a shortage of good food to eat because mother was so ingenious."

Despite their poverty, Mrs. Chisholm says she had "a wonderful childhood." She enjoyed school and feels that she received a good education in the New York schools. She adds, however, that this was before many of the current problems had developed, and she believes that a larger community role in the neighborhood schools is necessary if the current level of education in New York is to be improved.

Most of the congresswoman's unpleasant recollections are not related to the economic circumstances of the family, but to the indignities she suffered because of her race. A sensitive person, she was aware as a child that something was wrong around her. She began to sense that there was something different in the way teachers talked to black children, the way things were said, the way black children were handled.

"One time in Brownsville eleven neighborhood kids went to a ball game together," she recalls. "Four were Jewish kids and seven of us were black.

"As you know, children don't harbor racial discrimination. It is something they have to be taught. They play on their blocks together and have a good time until they are at an age when their parents begin to make them aware of the fact that some of them are white and the others are black.

"On this occasion we went to the ball game, laughing and happy together because for all of us it was a real treat. But when we got there and started to sit together the white kids were separated from us and put in another section, even though they didn't want to be. I'll never forget that. It was so humiliating that it sticks in my mind. I was only twelve at the time.

"When I got home I asked my parents about it, and all they would say was, 'You learn a lot when you get older.' They always had trouble explaining why blacks should be treated different from everyone else.

"Oh, yes, I felt the reaction of white toward black at a very early age. That is why I fight the way I do, and why I am so intense about what I am doing."

Mrs. Chisholm attended a girls' high school in the heart of Bedford-Stuyvesant. She was such an exceptional student that she got "all kinds of grants and scholarships." She enrolled in Brooklyn College and got her degree in social work, and then went on to Columbia University to earn a master's degree and professional diploma in the field of early childhood education.

After her graduation from Brooklyn College, Shirley began applying for employment, but met with many rebuffs. She had graduated cum laude, spoke well, dressed well, and had poise and confidence. Yet repeatedly, when she applied for jobs in competition with white classmates who were her intellectual and scholastic inferiors, they were hired and she was not. This embittered her because she knew that she was being rejected because she was black.

"When I was at Brooklyn College and in the debating society my professor suggested that I had leadership and speaking ability and that I should enter politics," Mrs. Chisholm says. "I forgot about it because I felt that blacks, and especially black women, essentially didn't have a chance.

"After I came out of college and became involved in the educational world I began to feel that I had to become involved. I was so angered by many things, and not just those things that had happened to me. Increasingly, as a teacher, people kept asking me to represent them and to become involved in volunteer civic work. I finally decided that I would have to fight the system, even if I had to stand alone."

That was twenty years ago, and she has been involved in politics ever since. Mrs. Chisholm was encouraged by her husband, Conrad, "a man who understood and understands me," and who saw in her a capacity for leadership. She, in turn, has also encouraged him.

Mr. Chisholm, when Shirley met him, was a waiter for the Horn and Hardart Company. Born in Jamaica, he was one of thirteen children of a village mayor. He had first come to the United States as a farm worker under the contract program, worked on farms in the Midwest, returned to Jamaica, and then was readmitted under an immigrant visa.

Mrs. Chisholm observed that her husband had an unusual faculty for remembering places and people, and encouraged him to enter the field of investigation and criminology. He enrolled in school, finished second in his class, and for nine years worked as a private detective. Then, two of his companions were killed while on duty, and Mrs. Chisholm became deeply concerned that her husband would meet a similar fate. She persuaded him to abandon his career as a detective, and he is now senior investigator for the New York City Department of Hospital Services.

Mrs. Chisholm was the first black woman elected to the New York State Assembly. She ran under the banner, "unbought and unbossed."

"I can say that perhaps I am the only unbossed and un-bought politician in Brooklyn," the congresswoman says. "I am in nobody's hip pocket and nobody gives me a lot of money to win an election. I probably ran the cheapest congressional election in this country this past year, and that money came from the people in my community."

Mrs. Chisholm says that any doubts she had about running for Congress were resolved early in the campaign when a man came to her door and handed her a crumpled envelope.

"Chisholm, this is the first," he said, and then disappeared.

Inside the envelope was $9.69, raised by people on welfare. Shirley cried a little over that contribution from people who could ill afford it, but before the campaign was over there were many more like it. The people in the community gave chitterlings parties, fashion shows, local teas, and resorted to every kind of fund-raising device to raise the twenty-eight thousand dollars that was spent in her behalf on both a hotly contested primary and a general election campaign against one of the outstanding figures in black leadership, James Farmer.

Mrs. Chisholm says she is "committed to nobody but the people," an attitude that is more than a little disturbing to the Democratic party power structure in New York City. The extent of her political independence was demonstrated most forcefully in the fall of 1969 when she supported Mayor John Lindsay for reelection over Mario Procaccino, the Democratic law and order candidate.

The congresswoman appeared with Mayor Lindsay at a press conference to announce her support of him and commented that while Lindsay had made mistakes, they were merely "tactical errors made in the quest of sound goals." Then, in a direct slap at her own party's candidate, she said:

"He (Lindsay) has attempted to shape and sustain a

city which is sensitive to the needs of all its citizens. He has appealed to our hopes rather than to our fears."

The congresswoman says that the Democratic party leaders, following her announcement of support for Lindsay, told her to resign her post as Democratic state committeewoman.

"I told them to bring me up on charges," she snaps. "I don't expect to hear any more about it."

Those who have followed Mrs. Chisholm's career say that she doesn't seem to know what fear is, and is that rare politician who, because of principle, is willing to stand alone and take the consequences. A devout Methodist, she says that her religion has been a major source of inner strength.

"The church has had a terrific influence in giving me stamina and strength," Mrs. Chisholm says. "When I am disillusioned all I have to do is get on my knees and pray, and in ten minutes I seem to have gotten a new lease on life. I get a kind of inner strength from God.

"I don't seem to need anybody to stand with me in what I do. The only thing I want and need and look to is my conscience—and God. I don't need crutches. I'm a very strong person.

"I am not here in the political arena out of a sense of political expediency. I am here out of a deep sense of the injustice done to my people. Everything that I do is based on the fact that I have a burning desire to fight for justice and equality for black people.

"I know that when I fight this way I am not going to be loved or accepted by certain forces. That does not bother me because as long as I do what my conscience tells me is right I know the people will continue to support me. When and if the people do not support me any longer I am quite willing to return to my profession, but while I am in politics I am not willing to let the people down."

The congresswoman says that she was rebellious as a

child, and always questioning and "as they say, talking out of turn." Her sisters would accept many things that she would not accept, and her mother found it necessary to control Shirley rather firmly. She says that if she were a teen-ager she would be in the forefront of their protest.

"I really believe that society is going to be saved by the women of America and the black and white students working together," she says. "There is more genuine concern about change among black and white students and women's groups."

Mrs. Chisholm, who is now forty-five, says that, when she was young, black people were "so complacent" and the whole atmosphere was different.

"There was a certain fear that stalked black people in this country for a long time," she says. "You knew you were supposed to be in your place, whatever that place meant. But after a few wars—black fellows coming back, not willing to take it any longer, being drafted and coming back to find that they can't get a house even if they have the money—the mood changed. I know that if I were young today I would be lashing out, also. I would not be engaging in violent destruction because I do not believe in violence, but I would be leading groups and mapping courses of action."

Congresswoman Chisholm believes that change will come only as the black power movement—which she sees as a constructive force—achieves its objectives.

"Black power is no different from any other kind of power," she says. "The only thing that gets people hung up is the adjective 'black.' If you didn't use that word 'black' in front of 'power' people wouldn't be so concerned about it. After all, people from different ethnic groups have sought power in this country throughout its history: first you had the Germans, then the Irish, and then the Italians.

"In the whole history of this country you have had the ascendancy of different ethnic groups from time to time.

The only thing that made them different was that they were white and nobody used the phrase 'white power.' Black power, as far as I am concerned, is the consolidation of the aims of the majority of people in the black society to realize that together, in spite of differences, we have common enemies to fight if we are going to emerge as a political and economic force to be reckoned with.

"It is a kind of coming together and making ourselves felt because of our blackness, because it is precisely our blackness that has been discriminated against in America."

Although Mrs. Chisholm often sounds bitter about the treatment accorded blacks by white society, she says that blacks must also set certain criteria for themselves, and not blame all of their ills on white people. She says that adult blacks must begin to set priorities for themselves and see that these priorities are passed on to their children.

"Education should be the number one priority," she says. "Every black home today should be discussing with their youngsters the importance and need for education. I know there are homes where there isn't enough to eat, and the rats are running all over, and the water bugs are fighting for space with the children. Perhaps these things seem of more immediate importance than the question of education, but if the children are to escape them they must have an education.

"And you can escape them. The lives of many of us who have made it out of poverty prove that it is possible if you have the will. But you have got to realize that the world has no room for weaklings, and that it is only weaklings who give up in the face of obstacles."

Young people who are not content with what they have, or with what their parents have had, must set goals for themselves and not be distracted from them, the congresswoman says. Today's world has no room for uneducated, untrained, unskilled people. In many situations you need a high school diploma even to push a broom.

10

John Shepherd

Bootstrap Businessman

Someone once asked John Shepherd how a man who had grown up in poverty because of discrimination against his color could escape becoming an angry black.

Shepherd, whose thriving Chicago enterprises have taken scores of families off the relief rolls and enabled many to buy their own homes, replied that he hasn't time to be an angry black because he is "too busy being an angry American."

The black entrepreneur takes a dim view of others of his race who want to develop a separate social and economic structure for black people in America. He has demonstrated to his own satisfaction, and to that of the 275 people who work for him, the capacity of blacks to compete within the American economic system.

"I think we should be proud of being black," Shepherd says, "but I don't think we need to spend all of our time telling ourselves so. I think we must think of ourselves as Americans first and blacks second.

"I believe in this country and its institutions, even though they have not delivered everything that the black population deserves. This is the greatest country in the world, and it does offer opportunity to those who have guts enough to get in there and fight for it. Certainly, it isn't as easy to get ahead if you have a black face, but that isn't an excuse for giving up on the system. If we have as much guts as our ancestors did, adversity should inspire us to fight to overcome it.

"Black men can make it in any field, but not just by sitting around telling themselves they are beautiful."

Shepherd, who is six foot four and weighs 210 pounds, acknowledges that many of his black friends, and his liberal white ones, disagree with his philosophy.

"They would call me an Uncle Tom, but I'm too big," he says with a grin. "They don't understand that I don't expect anything extra because I am black, but I also won't let anybody push me around *because* I am. When I'm right, I'll fight. It's like I once told a white union leader who didn't want to let my people into his union: 'If you can't work with me in this noble cause, perhaps I'll have more success with your successor.'"

Shepherd was brought up by a father who was never too poor to see that there was a dictionary, an encyclopedia, and a set of the Harvard Classics in his home. He read a great deal, and made his children read, and memorize, as well. All the Shepherd children, for example, were required to memorize Henley's *Invictus* before they were allowed to attend their first movie alone.

As a consequence of this training, Shepherd's conversation sparkles with quotations and passages from poetry that he recalls from his youth. He is also fond of illustrating his message with references to historical events.

"I like to think back to what I learned in school about American history," he says. "When I hear other blacks running down our political system, I remember how, during the Revolution, the country was defended by companies of Minutemen—farmers, tradesmen, ragtag and bobtail—that were held together by the regimental colors.

"I have never forgotten the story about the unit that retreated, leaving the standard bearer in the midst of the

enemy. Suddenly, his officer realized what had happened
and shouted, 'Bring the colors to us.'

" 'No,' replied the standard bearer. 'Bring the regiment
to the colors.'

"That's what I think blacks in America have to do. Bring
the regiment to the colors. Black awareness is fine, but
America was built on unity, and blacks have to find their
place in it in those terms. There's nothing basically wrong
with our system, and we shouldn't be tearing it down. We
should get in there and make it work for us."

Shepherd's attitude was profoundly influenced by his
father, who is now sixty-four and working as a supervisor
in the Chicago post office. The elder Shepherd, although
plagued all his life by poverty and illness, never allowed his
children to believe that a better life was not possible for
them.

"He always told us that for every man who will try to
hold you down there are ten who will help you if you
persevere," Shepherd recalls.

The turning point in Shepherd's life was a talk he had
with his family when he was only nine or ten. The family
was living on East 28th Street, in the heart of the Chicago
south-side ghetto, and John, in search of work that would
help the family make ends meet, applied for a job at a baby
crib factory located more than a mile away from his home.

The secretary who was in charge of the office hired him
as an office boy and he was overjoyed because he had been
job hunting for weeks. He had been working only a few
minutes and was about to go out to get coffee and dough-
nuts for the girls, when the man who owned the factory
came in and demanded to know what the little black boy
was doing there.

"About the time he was questioning her a white boy
walked into the office," Shepherd recalls. "She told her boss
that I was the new office boy, and he said, 'Oh no, he
isn't. You're going to hire that white boy over there.' He

pointed to the kid that had just walked in, gave me a nickel, and told me to go home."

John, so bitterly disappointed that he was in tears, ran the mile or more to his home. Sobbing, he told his mother what had happened and said, "Mamma, I hate all white folks."

His mother made no comment. She simply told him to go to his room. When John's father came home she recounted the story to him, and he went to John's room and sat down on the bed. He had the boy repeat to him what had happened.

"Then my father asked me to get the dictionary and he made me look up the word 'hate,'" Shepherd says. "When I had done so and read the definition aloud he made me look up the word 'consume.' Then he said, 'Always remember that hate consumes the hater, not the hated.'

"From that day on I was purged. It was one of the most beautiful moments of my life. I don't have any black-white hang-ups any more. Sure, I resent some of the slights I get, but it makes me proud to rise above them. I have learned that discrimination and prejudice are individual weaknesses, and I'm not handicapped by indiscriminate hatred of a whole group because of my feelings about an occasional individual within the group."

Shepherd, the youngest of five children, was born in Clarksdale, Mississippi, thirty-seven years ago. His father was a self-taught mechanic who dropped out of school after completing the seventh grade. He worked at the Clarksdale Ford Agency for $6.50 a week. Shepherd's mother, although she had attended college, worked at the Sunflower Laundry, earning only four dollars a week.

The family had very little money, but they did have a comfortable home with both plumbing and electricity. There was ample food, adequate clothing, and John's mother kept the family healthy with "castor oil and prayer." Their house was located in a neighborhood with unpaved streets, but it had a beautiful lawn and Shepherd still remembers that there was a pecan tree in front, a peach tree on the side, and a fig tree in the back.

Life in Clarksdale was pleasant, and his memories of it are of happy experiences within a closely knit family whose members had genuine love for one another. Their home was the center of activity for most of the kids in the neighborhood.

John and his two brothers and two sisters all had duties around the house. They were taught to share what they had, and developed mutual love and respect that even today is "very, very strong."

Mother Shepherd was very religious, so all the children went to Sunday school at the United Methodist Church. John developed a strong religious sense that still guides him today. At Christmas time, they sang all the traditional songs, and their father, who read avidly despite his limited education, delighted in reading aloud the familiar lines, "It was the night before Christmas, and all through the house . . ."

"We loved the story, and used to go to bed at night dreaming about sugar plums," Shepherd recalls. "Father explained what they were, but we never had any. We always had a Christmas tree, although some years it was kind of scrawny."

In 1938, when Shepherd was five, the family left the comfort and security of Clarksdale, and moved to Chicago. Unlike the modern migrants who leave the South for northern cities in search of a better job or a larger welfare check, the Shepherds left Clarksdale in the hope that a change in climate would improve the health of their daughter, Frances. She was asthmatic, and the doctor recommended the change, which he said might arrest the condition and lengthen her life.

When they arrived in Chicago the daughter's condition improved, but the family's went from bad to worse. They were able to rent a small apartment, but it was in a rundown neighborhood, and they had little to furnish it with. Mrs. Shepherd became ill, and could work very little. Her husband had difficulty finding work, and then, when he did get a job, became ill himself and frequently could not perform it.

At one point Mrs. Shepherd became so ill the doctor said she was dying. He would put her in the hospital if it would do any good, he said, but he felt that she wanted to die at home.

"My mother was a wonderful woman," Shepherd recalls. "I never knew her to utter a cross word or raise her voice. When we learned that she was dying, we all began to cry, except my grandmother. Instead, she began to pray, and I remember that she prayed that mother would live long enough so that the children would at least have learned to tell what was wrong and what was right. We saw a miracle happen. My mother came back and flourished and was an inspiration to all of us until her death in 1969."

When John's father became ill the family's already difficult situation became even more desperate, and the efforts of all the family members were required to keep body and soul together. Yet the father steadfastly refused to accept charity.

"I remember my dad turning down a bushel basket of food from the neighborhood precinct captain," Shepherd says. "I couldn't understand it, because we were hungry and really needed that food. My father told me that the man tried to give him the food in exchange for supporting a certain political party and that he had refused because he wouldn't sell his vote.

"I asked, 'Why didn't you take the food and vote for the one you wanted anyway?' Father replied that that would be lying, and he wouldn't compromise his dignity. He said that, once a man compromised and sold his right to be dignified, he sold his right to be a man."

John had a friend living a short distance away whose

father owned two grocery stores and four or five other buildings, and "was well off even by today's standards." The son, Ernest, always had many of the clothes that other children in the neighborhood lacked and envied—ear muffs, mackinaws, even high top boots that laced all the way to the top.

"I went down there one Thanksgiving day to play with him, and I saw more food than I had ever seen before in my life," Shepherd remembers. "They had turkey, ham, duck, and all the trimmings. I remember how good it smelled. There was even plum pudding.

"Ernest's mother invited me to stay and have dinner with them and, boy, how I wanted to, but I told her that if I didn't go home and eat the turkey and trimmings my mother was cooking, I'd get in Dutch.

"I left there, with the smell of all that food still lingering in my nostrils, and went home to a meal of boiled cabbage, boiled potatoes, and cornbread made without shortening. I was so choked up, thinking about the food that I had passed up, that I couldn't even eat. I finally left the table, ill, and went to my room.

"A little while later my mother came into my room to talk to me. I told her about the dinner they were having at Ernest's house, and how I had passed it up, and then something just snapped, and I really let go. I gave her a speech about all the things that Ernest had—ear muffs and boots and all—and there I was wearing tennis shoes with girls' stockings stuffed in them to keep my feet warm and a girl's dress under my pants for underwear so I wouldn't be cold when I went outside.

"My mother didn't say anything for a moment, just sat there looking kind of sad. I began feeling sorry that I had said anything because I knew they were giving me everything they could. But then, all of a sudden, she brightened up and said:

" 'But John, I'm praying for you! And look at your nose.

It isn't running and Ernest has already had whooping cough twice this year.'"

"Things were really rough in those days," Shepherd says. "But the times were difficult for almost everybody in the neighborhood; I guess we were all ragged.

"I was telling my daughters the other night that I could remember the high point of the summer when I was their age. It was to be able to have a popsicle. If I could just get one popsicle all summer long I felt my summer was made."

Shepherd began working when he was nine years old, and, while most of the money went to support the family, he was able to enjoy an occasional luxury and save a little money for himself. He earned his first money when he built a shoe-shine box and went into the streets to shine shoes. When he discovered that some of the other boys were either too lazy or too inept to make boxes of their own, he became an entrepreneur. He built two more boxes and leased them out to other boys. He may have been the first boy in America to get in the franchise business with shoe-shine boxes, and possibly the last.

At first Shepherd worked two days a week shining shoes but ultimately developed a schedule that kept him busy from the close of school in the afternoon until 9:30 at night, and all day long on Saturday. He earned about five dollars a week.

At the age of ten, Shepherd got a job in a grocery store working as a stock boy, delivery boy, and eventually as a butcher. When he was sixteen he bought the store. He was doing quite well at it, or thought he was, until an A&P market opened just down the street.

"It wasn't long before I discovered that all of my customers were credit customers and all the cash customers were going to the A&P," Shepherd says. "I was selling a lot of groceries, but it was all on the books. I finally had to fold, and I resolved then and there that I would be an independent businessman again, but not where I had to carry everything on credit in a 'Mom and Pop' type of store."

Meanwhile, Shepherd was continuing his education. He enjoyed school, and was particularly fond of the civics classes, history, and the subjects that dealt with government. The Civil War period was particularly fascinating to him, and he also became aware of some of the great early black figures in American history. His heroine was Sojourner Truth, the powerful black abolitionist, "because she typified the strength that is inherent in the Negro, and particularly in black women today."

Although none of the Shepherd children won college degrees, John says they all got as much college as they could. Shepherd had been attending college for two years when his only girlfriend, Edith, whom he later married, went to a dance and didn't invite him. He got even with her by joining the Army, and that ended college for him.

When Shepherd was released from the Army, where he had been attached to an intelligence unit, he was determined once again to have a business of his own. Shepherd does not share the feeling of some blacks that it is degrading to do manual work. He took his father's advice that any work that needs doing is worth doing, and worth doing well. He says work can be menial only if you do it so badly that you can't be proud of what you have done.

In 1957 he started the Venetian Blind Company, cleaning venetian blinds in apartment and office buildings. Before long the business grew into a contract janitorial service, and he obtained a contract with the New York Life Insurance Company to clean venetian blinds in the huge Lake Meadows apartment complex on Chicago's south shore.

"As soon as we took over at Lake Meadows, tenants began asking us to wash walls and windows, clean carpets, and do other heavy household maintenance chores," Shepherd says. "We did the work and were busy all the time, but I found that we weren't making any money in the process. I analyzed our activities and discovered that when my men finished cleaning they spent so much time rearranging furniture for housewives that the profit was eaten up by the extra time."

Concluding that it would be more profitable to concentrate on industrial accounts, Shepherd began soliciting building maintenance work from major Chicago firms. Many white executives were reluctant at first because they were dubious about the quality of service, dependability, and honesty of the black ghetto residents that Shepherd employed.

Through sheer persistence and supersalesmanship, Shepherd finally landed his first major industrial account, and the performance of his firm on that contract soon led to others. The new company was incorporated as the Dale Maintenance Company, the word "Dale" being an acronym made up of the first initials of his three daughters, Denise, Andrea, and Laurie, and that of Edith, his wife.

Shepherd operates on the theory that the more people he can employ, the more profit he can make, the more secure his company will be, and the more he can do to alleviate the impoverished condition of other blacks. He has expanded his operations as rapidly as he can recruit employees and train them to do the work.

The entrepreneur determined from the outset that he would not simply hire untrained people, hand them a mop, and turn them loose to clean washrooms and scrub floors. Instead, he has brought a new dignity to maintenance work by developing scientific techniques, using a wide variety of sophisticated compounds and chemicals that make maintenance a thoroughly professional job. The sparkling results please his customers and his employees as well. His employees need not consider themselves janitors or charwomen; they are technicians who employ skills in which they can take pride.

Shepherd established a hard-core training program long

before President Johnson enlisted corporate society in the widely publicized Jobs program for the ghetto unemployed. He has been recruiting in the ghetto for years, hiring blacks and whites alike. Many of his recruits were members of neighborhood gangs. Others had prison records or were on public assistance rolls. All he demands is that they agree with his Puritan philosophy: "We'll feed you if you're sick; otherwise you work."

His recruits receive classroom instruction in work habits, personal cleanliness, money management, and all of the specific skills that they need to perform professional maintenance work. They are paid wages above the prevailing scale and promoted rapidly as their skills increase.

A unique feature of Shepherd's agreement with the firms he services is a provision that enables his employees to aspire to jobs at an even higher level of skill. Shepherd reasoned that his workers, spending eight hours daily in industrial plants, would become acquainted with supervisors and other employees of the companies where they did their work. This, he concluded, would give them an advantage as candidates for employment by the firms with which he had contracts.

An employee of Shepherd's, working in the maintenance crew at Universal Oil Products Company, is interviewed for employment with that company after he has been working in the plant for a year. If he is found to be qualified for a more responsible position with that firm, Shepherd cheerfully releases him to UOP.

Many of his employees have established themselves in lifetime careers through this process. The first to make it was a lady who had been on Aid to Dependent Children, began working for Shepherd cleaning floors, advanced to shift supervisor, and then went to work for the firm whose floors she had been scrubbing as receptionist at the front desk in their general office building.

"I have refused to take any federal money to operate our

training program although there are programs that would reimburse us for the entire training costs," Shepherd says. "I ask the people who work for me to raise themselves by their own bootstraps, and I want to set the example of proving to them that I can also raise myself by mine.

"Refusing the government money is our own little sign that we don't need to take handouts from anybody, and neither do they. We have helped scores of people get off the welfare rolls, and many of them have gone on to buy their own homes.

"When the trainees enter our class, I start them off by telling them that their philosophy should be 'Don't give me a dime, just give me a chance.' I tell them that the greatest enemy black people have is welfare—welfare that doesn't help people, but simply keeps them from helping themselves.

"I really believe that. I can't think of a better weapon for a white supremacist than to give black people just enough money to keep them alive, so that they lose any incentive to improve the condition that they are in."

Many of Shepherd's customers feared that they would experience an increase in pilferage because of the criminal backgrounds and desperate poverty of many of those whom he recruits. In practice, the reverse has been the case. Shepherd indoctrinates his employees so thoroughly on the virtues of honesty, and their obligation to help the company grow so that others can be employed, that he has yet to receive the first report of a theft by one of his workers.

One of his most prized possessions is a letter from a secretary in one of the offices his people service. She wrote:

"Dear Mr. Shepherd:

"I would appreciate it very much if you would dispose of the enclosed ballpoint pen. It is worn out and I have thrown it in the wastebasket every day for the past week, but each morning I find that your maintenance woman has placed it back on my desk."

"That wonderful employee of ours was so determined not to be accused of taking anything that even appeared to be of value that she wasn't taking the slightest chance," Shepherd chuckles.

In addition to his maintenance company, Shepherd also operates an industrial security company that provides plant protection and building security, and a drywall construction company that does subcontract work for other construction firms.

"I have 270 employees, many of them white, doing things together," he says. "We have steadfastly adhered to the concept that this is what America is all about.

"I also think it is what black power is all about. Every time I do a good job, or my employees do a good job, it helps defeat the crumbling lie that blacks can't produce or be counted on in times of strife.

"Look at what we are accomplishing in our various firms. Thirty-two percent of my employees are white. White people working with us, looking to us for their welfare, their payroll check—that's black power. But it is also American power, black and white people, working together, and getting ahead."

Shepherd says that, like Cyrano, he "likes to climb the windmill of chance and reach for the stars." He takes only a modest salary from the business, and his family still lives in an eighteen-thousand-dollar home they bought several years ago. The profits are poured back into the business and Shepherd works eighteen or nineteen hours a day, mostly on expansion plans.

He hopes to expand his operation throughout the country, training and creating new jobs for the poor: "black people, white people, brown people, and red people."

"We plan to build homes," he says. "We are going to give people who lack training and haven't been able to work the training they need so they can hold steady jobs. We are hiring people now and sending them to various schools. We're not going to let anyone tell us that we can't have our own plumbers, and electricians, and carpenters. We're going to train black people to do these jobs, and I can't imagine myself letting anybody, a labor leader or anyone else, tell me that I can't do something because I'm black or our employees can't do something because they're black."

Despite his conviction that individual blacks must control their own destiny, Shepherd is militant in his belief that black people must work together to force action by other elements of society to make the American system work for everyone. He has a low regard for most of the black politicians who have gained power in the past, but great respect for some of the young black voices that are being heard today.

"I look at the discord on the college campuses and among the children—the youngsters asking questions and just raising general hell—and I don't wring my hands over it," he says. "I'd rather steal a phrase from Churchill and say that when all this dies down a thousand years from now the historians will say that this was America's finest hour.

"We have some young men now—men like Jesse Jackson and Julian Bond—who may not always be right, but who are turning the lights on in the dark corners of the nation's ghettos and saying to a complacent society, 'Open your eyes now, and look at this.'

"They're making themselves heard, and I think white Americans are starting to look and listen. If black Americans will prepare themselves to take advantage of it, I believe that the American society of the future will have a dignified and rewarding place in it for them."

11

Manford Byrd

Boss of Chicago's Schools

Manford Byrd is the chief operating officer of the second largest school system in America. As deputy superintendent of the Chicago public schools, he manages the day-to-day operations of six hundred schools, supervises some twenty-five thousand teachers, and is responsible for the education of nearly six hundred thousand children. At his disposal is a budget of half a billion dollars a year.

That Byrd should rise to the most responsible and demanding post in public education held by any black in America is something of a paradox. His father was sixty-three years old before he learned to read and write!

The Chicago educator came from childhood circumstances as deprived as those of the poorest children who attend his schools today. He was born in Bruton, Alabama, a sawmill town about halfway between Montgomery and Mobile, and except for a brief period spent in nearby Fishpond, Alabama, he lived there until he went away to college. Bruton was a community of about five thousand, dominated by the T. R. Miller Mill Company, which literally owned the town.

The mill owners provided housing for their white employees, who paid little or no rent, but not for the workers who were black. They lived nearby in flimsy rented houses owned by a local tycoon. The black workers put in long hours for low pay and for most of them it was a desperate struggle to pay the rent.

Byrd's father was a laborer in the mill, and when things were slack he and the other blacks were the first to be laid off. In those emergencies he maintained his family by doing odd jobs and working in the forest with a turpentine gang. His earnings were always minimal, and in order to support their five children, Mrs. Byrd also worked, as a maid.

"Dad just didn't have what it took to get a better job," Byrd says. "He was not able to articulate the reasons, but mother was. She told us that if we were going to have a better life we had to get an education, to *be* somebody, and that it would take hard work. Mother had been to grade school, but not to high school, and it was she who felt the need for us to have an education, who urged us to go, who insisted that we go and that we do well in school.

"She worked very hard, but no matter how tired she was she would go to PTA meetings, because she wanted to know how we were doing and behaving. My only sister died in infancy, but I had two brothers and my mother was always behind all three of us, pushing. She whipped us when it was necessary.

"Dad would ask us now and then if we had done our homework, but he didn't take the same interest mother did, and at any rate he worked so hard and long that we didn't see as much of him. He left early in the morning and stayed late at night, and much of the time he was working seven days a week. He was illiterate, and it wasn't until about six years ago that he went back to school and learned to read and write."

The neighborhood in which Bruton's poor blacks lived had no sidewalks—just dirt trails—and the roads were also just dirt. Byrd's house was built of weather-beaten boards, with three rooms, two of which had fireplaces. An old wood

stove was used for cooking, and it was one of young Manford's regular chores to gather kindling for the stove and
wood for the fire that heated the wash pot in the back yard.
The house had no sanitary facilities—only an outhouse—
and their water came from an outdoor pump.

"Dad was rather passive in the sense that he let mother
run the house and manage the children and considered it
his obligation to go out and get things for the family," Byrd
recalls. "We had no regular money. I can recall dad going
out on odd jobs and coming home with a gallon of cane
juice, which was a real luxury. Sometimes he would be paid
in syrup and we would have syrup and corn bread.

"Those were real treats because our food was nothing
elaborate and often there wasn't much of it. Sometimes
when we were at our meal and about to run through a
short supply dad would be out in the yard and mother
would call to him and say, 'You'd better come in before
these boys eat everything here.' He would reply, 'Let 'em
eat; I'm happy to see them eat.' I often wondered how he
could be delighted with three guys about to eat him out
of house and home, not leaving enough for him. Later I
realized that he was always missing on the days when there
wasn't enough to go around. He just wanted to be sure
we had enough and stayed out of sight so we wouldn't have
to share an inadequate supply with him."

The Byrds raised chickens, so sometimes they ate one of
them, and for many years they always kept a couple of pigs.
Byrd's father had made an arrangement with several board-
ing houses to collect their garbage. The boy picked it up
with his wagon, and the garbage provided much of the diet
for the hogs.

"We killed the hogs in January and dressed them out
and salted and smoked the meat," Byrd says. "Nothing
was wasted. Mother made sausage and she used the fat to
make shortening and from that we had the cracklings that
were used to make crackling bread. We had, chitterlings, of

course, and black-eyed peas and lots of greens. Milk was a rare commodity; there was no regular diet of milk."

The family bought very little clothing, and what was purchased was passed down from the oldest son to the younger brothers, if it did not wear out along the way. Other families gave them clothing that they had outgrown.

"I knew that I couldn't get the things I wanted the way some other kids could," Byrd said. "I knew that I couldn't look to mother and dad to buy things because they were having such a struggle to pay the rent. I felt it was up to me to do what I could in the way of odd jobs. I guess maybe I was encouraged in this by the fact that there were many other kids in the neighborhood with the same drive. Some of them were worse off than we were because they were living with a single parent. I remember one boy on the street who lived with his mother and was out working all the time. I told myself that if he could do it, I could, too.

"I worked at all kinds of odd jobs, mowed lawns, knocked down pecans in the fall of the year, picked berries, and stacked peanuts—anything I could do to bring in a quarter or a dollar here and there. I got a job in my sophomore year in high school as a janitor at one of the popular barbershops that was owned by a black but had a clientele that was white. I had the concession of selling newspapers and polishing shoes in exchange for doing the custodial work in the shop. Easily half of what I earned went to help support the family, and the rest went for school. The only time I recall splurging and spending some money was in my junior year in high school when I got to go to Montgomery to a football game."

Although Byrd and his brothers did not have much as children, and worked hard for what little they had, ignorance of what they lacked kept them from brooding about it. They also had an advantage denied to many city children today—the warmth of a home filled with love, and the companionship and guidance of both of their parents.

"My brothers and I didn't feel put upon because we had to sleep three in a bed," he says. "I can remember on some of those cold nights it was fun to say, 'Let's go to bed and let's bundle up because it's going to be cold back there.' We slept in the room that had no fireplace and it *was* cold, but we kidded about who was going to get caught in the middle, and what could have been misery became a happy game. We reveled in simple pleasures, as when dad got some peanuts from a farmer to parch on the fire in the evening before we went to bed. Those were all happy moments as I recall them."

Byrd's older brother was enthusiastic about school, and his conversation about the things he was doing made the younger boys eager to advance to the upper grades. Byrd and his schoolmates were also quite competitive, and, if one achieved something, the others would try to top it.

The graduation from high school of their oldest son was the major event in his parents' lives, and they established a family tradition, carefully putting away the white shirt he wore. It was a sentimental thing, but it was also a clever motivational device, for they told the younger boys that if they graduated from high school the shirt would be waiting for them to wear.

"We admired and respected our older brother, and they were challenging us to fill his shirt instead of his shoes," Byrd says. "No one had to tell me that school was the next day. I looked forward to it and really wanted to go."

Byrd attended the public schools in Bruton through his sophomore year and then enrolled in Southern Normal High, a parochial school administered by the Reformed Church in America, an affiliate of the Dutch Reformed Church. Although his father was not active in the church, his mother attended faithfully, and insisted that the children make a weekly appearance in Sunday school. Manford also participated in an after-church organization for young people, the Baptist Training Union.

It was customary for the parochial school to hold an annual youth conference during which classes were dismissed for a week while leaders in education, religion, and other fields counseled with the students on goals and issues. At one of these conferences Byrd met a minister who urged him to attend a college also affiliated with the church.

Byrd had a burning desire to go on to college, but had never set his sights on anything other than one of the nearby schools—Alabama State or Talladega. He didn't even know how he was going to swing that. Two or three weeks later the minister wrote him and said some information was being sent to him by Iowa Central College in Pella, Iowa.

Although Byrd was interested in going to Iowa to school, the cost was beyond his reach, and he wrote the minister that he did not have enough money to enroll. He was advised that since his grades were very good—he was second in his class—he would be awarded a scholarship.

Byrd felt the need to cut himself loose from his family and friends and prove to himself that he could make it on his own, so he enrolled at Iowa Central. He waited on tables and did odd jobs to supplement the scholarship, and one of his professors allowed him the use of a washing machine so that he could wash his own clothes. In his second year he had a roommate who had learned to do dry cleaning in the Army. He agreed to do Byrd's cleaning if Byrd would wash his clothes—an arrangement that helped both of the boys to conserve their limited money supply.

"As I went along my finances got progressively tighter because the tuition kept going up," Byrd recalls. "I finally wound up playing basketball and baseball and applying for an athletic scholarship, too. When I graduated I had the academic scholarship, an athletic scholarship, waited on tables two meals a day, and in order to graduate finally had to borrow $150 from the college to complete my obligations there."

Even as a small child Byrd had been so impressed with

the importance of education that he wanted to become a teacher. He was also influenced by the fact that, except for a mortician and a dental technician, the only black success models in Bruton were either preaching or teaching school.

Byrd began his teaching career in Quincy, Illinois, and taught there for five years. He regards this decision, along with his decision to attend school in Iowa, as the major turning points in his life.

"I could have attended school close to home, or gone back home to teach," he says, "but I deliberately chose to study and to work where I had no relatives and friends, and would have to make them all. It was a wise decision because I could apply myself totally to study and work, without being distracted by social life.

"By the end of the third year it became obvious to me that I needed to be in a larger educational center in order to continue my studies and broaden my career as a teacher. I had been attending summer school at Atlanta University, working on my master's degree, and needed the library facilities that were available in a larger city. I applied to several of the big city school systems and heard from Chicago right away."

Byrd passed the examination for a teacher's certificate in Chicago, and began teaching sixth grade at Howland school in September, 1954. The school was on the west side, in the heart of the Lawndale neighborhood. The community, now one of Chicago's most depressed areas, was already in the midst of transformation into an all-black ghetto. He spent eight years there, meanwhile earning his master's degree, and became a master teacher and an assistant principal before taking the examination for principal in 1962. He passed it and was assigned as principal to the Goethals school, which is in Englewood, another black neighborhood.

During his years as a teacher in ghetto schools, Byrd had become increasingly concerned over the youngsters in their early and middle teens who had dropped out of school, lacked the skills for decent employment, and appeared to be headed for personal tragedy. When he arrived at Goethals he decided to experiment with an innovative program designed to encourage dropouts to return and finish school.

Byrd opened a Vocational Guidance and Educational Center in an abandoned telephone company building. The center concentrated on youngsters between fourteen and sixteen years of age who had met with failure in school because of their difficulty in adjusting to it and who, in many cases, had been in trouble with the law, as well. All of those who enrolled were told that they were on the threshold of entering high school, regardless of the grade level they had previously achieved. They would be admitted to high school if they applied themselves and mastered basic reading, writing, and mathematics skills.

The students were given concentrated programs of instruction in these subjects, under highly motivated teachers who transmitted their enthusiasm to their pupils. They worked in small groups, in an environment that bore no resemblance to the traditional classroom teaching situation. They worked hard, motivated by the prospect of entering high school without the embarrassment of attending grade school classes with children much younger than themselves. Byrd says that the program "gave many young people a new lease on life."

Byrd continued to rise rapidly in the Chicago school system. He became principal of the Juliet Lowe Upper Grade Center in the Englewood community, and then principal of Englewood High School. In June, 1967, he was appointed assistant to the general superintendent of schools, and in December, 1968, was named deputy superintendent.

Managing the day-to-day operations of a school system responsible for educating well over half a million children is an enormous responsibility, and a source of great satisfaction to Byrd. He sees it as an opportunity to contribute to the educational development of all of the city's school children, to strive for the improvement of urban educational programs, and to help accelerate the progress of his own race.

"I sit in many conferences and councils that affect black people," he says, "and because I know the aspirations and feelings of blacks I can contribute a point of view that most black people will share. Moreover, as I administer the school system, I can ask the right questions about areas in which I think we are not making enough progress."

Despite the complaints about some urban ghetto schools, Byrd says that the education available to black children in the Chicago school system is superior to that which gave him the foundation to reach the position he now holds.

"Most of the criticisms of educational quality deal with the relevance of traditional instructional programs to the employment opportunities in a technological age," he says, "or result from comparison of city schools with the lavishly financed schools in the suburbs. The fact is that any child who applies himself can get an excellent education in the Chicago schools."

Byrd acknowledges, however, the need to make urban education more relevant to existing job opportunities so that children can see the relationship between what they are learning and the careers that lie ahead. The basic problem, he says, is money.

"I do not believe," he says, "that the public schools, with the limited financing available to them, will be able to equip themselves to train students for today's job market. We need the help of the business community to provide equipment, and to work with us on work-study programs in which students can begin, while in school, the job training that will prepare them for the careers that they will take up when they graduate from high school."

Byrd believes that programs of this sort will also provide the motivation needed to encourage young people to stay in school because they will be able to see the relationship between what they are learning and a productive adult career. Chicago is launching an "urban high school" to experiment with this type of program.

Another weakness of urban schools, according to Byrd, is the lack of communication between the school and the people of the neighborhood it serves. In smaller cities and suburban neighborhoods parents take a more active interest in school affairs, and the school often is a center of community activity.

"If we are going to motivate children in the early grades more effectively, the indigenous people of the neighborhood must be brought into closer contact with the school," he says. "They must become involved in its affairs so that the school is seen as a part of the community—indeed, as an extension of it. Then it will be spoken of as an institution that can help people, not as an enemy. If people see the school as something that is part of their lives, as something that will contribute to their standard of living, as something that has produced the success images that they see, it will mean more to them. The children will want to attend, and their parents will be encouraged to see that they attend."

While Byrd believes that education and training must be the foundation of black progress, as they have been for the progress of all ethnic groups in America, he also believes that the current thrust to increase economic and political strength in the black community is a worthy objective.

"Black power means a lot of different things to different people," he asserts, "but I believe that it can be constructive if it means self-reliance, or the use by a group of its economic power to help improve the lot of the group and the individuals within it.

"I do not believe, however, that under the guise of 'black power' we should promote any feelings of hate because of the deprivation, the degradation, and the discrimination that blacks have experienced in this country. It is self-defeating to do so because if we spin our wheels and use our energy in hating others we will only destroy ourselves.

"So, if black power comes under that guise I want to identify it and I want to reject it. If it means a kind of separatism, I want to reject that. But if it means pride in blackness, if it means getting political strength and wielding it in ways that will lead to the improvement of the services that blacks need and that other people already have, if it enhances the economic position of the black population, I'm for that."

Byrd says that if he were a teen-ager today he, too, would be militant in trying to accelerate the progress of his race. The civil rights legislation enacted in the past decade has made it possible for black people to voice the protests that they once dared not reveal. Open discussion of racism and the mistreatment accorded blacks throughout most of America's history has made black children angry about what happened to their ancestors and what is happening to them.

The educator says that most young blacks are determined to do something about their situation, but have not always clearly defined their goals. He is concerned that their tactics and their proposed solutions are not always the kind that will really solve their problems.

"I think one of the things that bothers me most is the tendency of many of the younger militants—those who are sixteen, seventeen, eighteen—to see themselves as sacrificial lambs," he says. "They are still in their teens, but they are saying, 'Well, it's all over for us and whatever we can do will make it better for our younger brothers and sisters who are only five or six.' It is tragic for a youngster to be copping out or dropping out of the competition when he's still got fifty years to live.

"These kids have got to be convinced that it isn't all over

for them. They have got to be convinced that opportunities today, while still not good enough, are much, much greater and are increasing all the time. They must be shown that the blacks who are building an enduring and profitable and respected place for themselves in society are the ones who are prepared to take advantage of the opportunities when they come."

Byrd shares with many other successful blacks a real concern that too many black children, particularly those who have been denied the guidance of a stable home environment, are trying to emulate models that give an illusory appearance of success. They see the gangsters, the policy pushers, and even the crooked politicians who wear three hundred dollar suits, drive fancy automobiles, and always seem to have unlimited money to spend, and conclude that this is the easy way out of the poverty-stricken circumstances that they are in. Byrd was stunned last year when one of his brighter student leaders told him that his ambition in life was to be a pimp.

"It isn't easy to persuade those kids that the appearance of success which is based on activities that are outside the law is a transient thing," Byrd says. "It is tragic that many of them can't be persuaded, and learn their lesson the hard way, by going to jail."

The black educator has some strong personal reasons for concern about the directions taken by young people of his race. He has three sons of his own, one nine, one six, and one who is only a year old. He does not allow the burden of his responsibilities to other Chicago school children to keep him from counseling and motivating his own. He talks to the two older boys about the things that concern them at their age, and tries to encourage them in what they are doing in school.

"I try to point out that if they are doing something at all they should try to do it well," he says. "I tell them that they should attach importance to completing every task that they undertake. I try to encourage their love of reading, and to raise the kinds of questions that will require them to learn for themselves, or to develop a skill.

"As they grow older I will try to make them appreciate what I have learned for myself—that young people must recognize that they are the vital part of the formula that will lead to their own success or failure. Outside forces—discrimination, for example—may sometimes limit the kinds of opportunities that will be open to them, but opportunities will always be there if they are prepared to take advantage of them.

"The youngster who develops his skills and believes that he *can* succeed and be somebody *will* succeed and be somebody. But learning isn't easy. He must apply himself, study, sacrifice, do the important things until it hurts. It will be hard for him to work while his friends are playing. What he must remember is that it takes only a few years of hard work when he is young to avoid a lifetime of the hardest kind of menial work when he grows up."

12

Gwendolyn Brooks

Poet Laureate

Gwendolyn Brooks is one of God's gentle creatures, as befits a lady with poetry in her soul and kindness in her heart. Yet much of the literary work that brought her the Pulitzer Prize in 1950 has a sting in its message that was born of her bitter experiences as a black American child.

The black poet's story is that of a shy and withdrawn youngster who says she is just beginning to live—through her work with young people—at the age of fifty-two. When she was four, Gwendolyn liked to sit on her back porch and contemplate the clouds, a pastime that she finds fascinating to this very day. The porch was that of their home on the south side of Chicago—a house that her father purchased after bringing his family from Topeka, Kansas, where the future poet was born.

Although they were buying their home, Miss Brooks recalls her childhood circumstances as "very poor."

"We were not bottom-of-the-barrel poor," she says. "My father did have a job as a janitor and later as a shipping clerk for the McKinley Music Company. But life was a constant struggle, and while the house was a great source of comfort to the family the possibility of losing it was a constant threat."

"That house did mean a lot to me," Miss Brooks recalls,

a wistful look coming into her eyes. "It was on two floors, and quite large, so we usually rented out the second floor. The characters in some of my poems lived upstairs. The house had a front yard and a back yard which were very neat and well-kept, and my mother planted flowers there.

"It was mother's pride that she took very good care of us. She fed us well, and we always put on clean clothes in the afternoon. After dinner we were allowed to play with the children in the neighborhood, but not for very long. One of the poems I wrote, 'A Song In the Front Yard,' is about my resentment at having to come in behind the gate before the other children had to on summer evenings."

Gwendolyn and her younger brother had rooms to themselves. Hers was tiny, but it contained her most prized possession—a desk which her father gave her when she was thirteen.

"It had a lot of tiny compartments, and what a thrill it was the night that it arrived," she says. "I wrote at it for years and have it to this day."

During the Depression Gwendolyn's father had a hard time getting work. He was laid off from his job at the music company, and only occasionally was he able to get part-time jobs.

"They were always poorly paid, and we resorted to beans, but I can't say I really suffered," Miss Brooks recalls. "I knew we didn't have all the things that some other people had, but we were a very happy family. I never put a lot of stress on clothes—still don't—and I didn't brood or grieve. Our house was poorly furnished and it bothered my mother when people came, but it wasn't too bad."

Gwendolyn was so bashful in school that she didn't enter into social activities, and she remembers that when she left school each day it was with a great feeling of relief. She had average grades, but she read a lot and was encouraged to do so by her parents, particularly her mother, who had been a teacher in Topeka. They believed that education was the key to life, had a reverence for books, and kept the Harvard Classics in the house.

When she entered high school in Hyde Park, Gwendolyn became very conscious of the problems she was to encounter because of her race. There was a great deal of prejudice at the school, "nothing overt, but a sort of coldness and controlled hostility among some of the white children who had never met black children except those of their servants."

Some of the teachers were also very cold and withdrawn, which seemed almost threatening to a sensitive child. Not all of them behaved in that manner, however. Miss Brooks recalls a journalism teacher named Margaret Anderson who encouraged her greatly, and she has been looking for her ever since. There was also a history teacher at Englewood High School, Ethel Hearn, who was very encouraging.

Gwendolyn had expected that high school would be more exciting than the lower grades, but for the most part she hated it. She stuck with it because she knew how important it was, and found comfort and self-expression in the poetry that she wrote.

Gwendolyn had begun writing poetry when she was seven. Her mother immediately decided to nurture the talent, and her father also encouraged her. He read poems and sang songs to Gwendolyn and her brother. Although she was very young, the child began to know and love the black poets—James Weldon Johnson and Langston Hughes —and all of the white poets whom her father read.

The family belonged to the Metropolitan Community Church, where her mother taught Sunday school and sometimes played the piano to accompany the hymns. Gwendolyn always recited in the Easter and Christmas programs until she was thirteen or fourteen.

When she was about fifteen the budding poet discovered an anthology that contained the work of many black poets. She became very excited at the discovery that so many black people were writing poetry.

This revelation, coupled with the experience she had gained since she was thirteen by publishing a mimeographed community newspaper called the *Champlain Weekly News,* probably solidified her decision to become a poet. She liked writing poetry, but didn't like journalism because that kind of writing seemed to her to be nothing but work. At about the same time the black poets, Hughes and Johnson, visited Chicago and Gwendolyn heard them speak and spoke to them. From that day forward there was no turning back from poetry as her career.

Gwendolyn attended Wilson Junior College, graduated in 1936, and continued to write. She says there were never any serious obstacles in her path—that people who helped her had more trouble than she did.

"I've sent material to magazines and publishers that was returned, but when it came back it was simply because it wasn't good enough," she says. "One man in a literary competition who awarded me prizes three years in a row was finally fired because of his predilection for giving prizes to Negroes."

Miss Brooks has had a career as an instructor in creative writing at a number of schools—most recently at Northeastern Illinois State College and the University of Wisconsin—but at the end of the 1968-69 school year she abandoned teaching to devote all her time to her literary work.

The poet has done many books and is always at work on another. Her first to be published was *A Street In Bronzeville* in 1945. It was her second book, *Annie Allen,* that won the Pulitzer Prize, but the most popular of her works has proved to be another—*Bronzeville Boys and Girls.*

Miss Brooks is married and has a son twenty-eight, and a daughter seventeen. The daughter, a sophomore at the University of Illinois, also has writing talent but is not inclined to develop it because, having watched her mother, she considers it too hard a job. The son, who is likewise talented, expects to do something with his writing skills.

The black poet "went natural" in 1969. She says she changed her hair style on George Washington's birthday, in memory of the story about the cherry tree and the little boy who could not tell a lie.

"It was a very exciting thing to do, and I must say I feel honest," she says.

The new hairdo is perhaps more a symbol of change in attitude that has been coming over the once-shy black girl. Her writing—in poems such as "Riots"—is taking a more militant tone. That poem deals with the fear that is in a mythical liberal white aristocrat named John Cabot when confronted by a mob of angry young blacks.

"I wrote it during the riots that followed Dr. King's assassination," Miss Brooks says. "'A riot is the language of the unheard,' he said. After that riot I saw a photo in the paper of a throng of young men in their teens coming down the street—half a page devoted to this picture—and they looked so alive and so annunciatory. It occurred to me to wonder how a certain kind of young white man faced with such a throng and faced with his own confrontation with his own innards would react.

"I think the poem speaks to the times because it deals with the many whites, both young and old, who think they are liberal but they're not. They are just as cold and hostile inside—deep inside and sometimes not so deep—as many of the people who are outright in their wickedness."

"I don't see how anyone who is decent and just can be against black power," the poet insists. "Nobody gets excited about white power, and black power merely means that black people who have been weak and helpless for so long will no longer be so. I'm all for that.

"I'm not frightened by these cruel words that people use. The word militance—that doesn't bother me. When people who are frightened by the word use it they are merely talking about those young people who are no longer willing to stand what was stood by many of their elders. And, once again, I'm all for them.

"I am not for killing; I don't like the idea of killing or violence. But I do believe that we must forge ahead and do something to relieve our circumstances."

Miss Brooks says that when she was a teen-ager she "didn't take any course" with respect to the problems of her race, but neither did her friends.

"Then the militants were Walter White and Roy Wilkins," she recalls. "Wilkins was quite eloquent as the editor of *The Crisis*. We are indebted to them for what they have accomplished, but I think if I were a teen-ager today I would be doing exactly what the more strong-minded teen-agers are doing."

"These young people are having an effect on white society," the poet maintains. "Young black people are having an effect on young white people. It is very exciting to watch them insisting on what they should have. As for what is happening on the campuses—I think all such outbursts are creative.

"The government, churches, and businesses had better wake up. We are going to have more anarchy, if you want to call it that, unless there is a general awakening."

The lady poet, who two years ago succeeded the late Carl Sandburg as "Poet Laureate" of Illinois, is always ready to lend encouragement to young black writers who are emerging as young men and women of promise in the literary field.

In 1969 she announced that she would award, through *Negro Digest*, two annual prizes of $250 each for the best poem and the best short story published by a black author during the year.

Miss Brooks tells black youngsters not to try to make it as white poets.

"I suggest that they write and write and write and read

and read and read, whether black, white, or yellow," she says. "Black writers no longer have any trouble making it because of color—black and white publishers are eager to publish their work.

"I work with young people whenever they will allow me to, but you can't put a leash on them and lead them around. You help them as they want you to and when they want you to.

"I think the most exciting part of my life is right now, not because of my literary work but because of the work I am doing with young people."

13

John H. Johnson

Pioneer Publisher

John Johnson's offices are in an abandoned mortuary, but even in jest it could not be said that he heads a dying enterprise. He is, in fact, the most successful black publisher in the world. Nor does his stature have to be measured in a limited competition within his own race. It is conspicuous even when compared with the white giants of magazine publishing—DeWitt Wallace of *Reader's Digest*, Gardner Cowles of *Look*, the late Henry Luce of *Life*.

From his office in the fading splendor of the one-time mortuary situated on the edge of Chicago's south side ghetto, Johnson presides over a publishing empire that produces four magazines, with a combined circulation of 3,500,000 copies a month. The income from *Ebony, Negro Digest, Jet*, and *Tan*, combined with that from other interests which include a cosmetics firm and the largest single holding in the Supreme Life Insurance Company, has made him a millionaire. *Ebony* alone produces about eight million dollars in advertising revenue every year.

Some of Johnson's readers complain that his publications are not militant enough, but their nervously energetic fifty-one-year-old publisher scoffs confidently at his critics.

"I think you can be militant in anything you do," he says. "Booker T. Washington is somewhat out of favor with young blacks today, but I still recall a conversation he had with an old friend whom he met when he returned, after twenty-five years, to the place of his birth. Washington asked the friend what he had been doing all those years.

" 'Have you raised a family?'

" 'No,' the friend replied.

" 'Do you have a job?'

" 'No.'

" 'Are you active in community affairs?'

" 'No,' the friend said again. 'Frankly, Dr. Washington, I've been so busy trying to solve the race problem that I haven't had time to do anything else.' "

Johnson, after telling the story, pauses for a moment to let the point sink in, and then continues:

"Militancy to me does not mean protesting. I think young people can choose a target, choose a career, and be militant in that career. They can insist that there be absolute equality in it, and press and fight for it. Militancy to me means active participation in bringing about whatever goal you are trying to achieve.

"If I had my life to live over I would live it the same way, if I were permitted to do so. I would live it in a militant way and I think I have lived it in a militant way.

"Militancy may mean moving forward, fighting for complete equality, and taking advantage of all the opportunities. It does not necessarily mean destroying all of the existing institutions without building new ones."

Johnson maintains that the development of successful black businesses is the most effective way to develop black power. He cites an experience he had with a printer in the early years when he was still struggling, with severely limited resources, to get his publishing enterprise under way.

"When I first began doing business with this printing firm the man who was president then, and is now dead, used to call me up and say, 'John, this is Mr. So-and-So. I would like to see you in my office tomorrow morning at nine o'clock.' I was behind in my bills and I was not doing too well financially, so I'd rush over to see this man because I knew I needed him.

"Five or six years passed, all of my bills were paid, I had money in the bank and my business was doing well, and my contract with him was about to expire. Now this same printer called up and said, 'Mr. Johnson, this is Charlie calling. May I come over to see *you* in *your* office at *your* convenience?'

"This, in my opinion, is an example of black power. After I became successful this man knew I had the power. He respected it and so, without any coaching from me, he acted the way he should have been acting all along. He paid me the same kind of courtesy he would have paid any other man with power, whether the power was black, or yellow, or any other color."

Johnson was born in Arkansas City, Arkansas, on January 19, 1918. His father, a sawmill worker, was killed in an accident when John was six. His mother, who was employed as a domestic in the home of a white physician, later married another worker from the same mill.

The Johnsons lived in a three-room frame house without indoor plumbing—a shortcoming that did not trouble them particularly because in all of Arkansas City there was only one black family that had a bathroom in their house.

John ate the usual "soul food" diet, rarely had any spending money, and always wore hand-me-downs. Yet, despite their poverty, the Johnsons were never on welfare in Arkansas, because at that time there was no such thing as welfare for black people in the South. When a family experienced unusual difficulties the neighbors would "chip in and help."

It was not until John ventured outside his all-black neighborhood at the age of five or six that he became aware of the color of his skin.

"I went into a drug store," he recalls, "and the clerk

stared at me coldly and said, 'What do you want, black boy?' in a very mean and unpleasant tone. In those days 'black' didn't have the pleasant connotations it does today. It was a very derisive term. I knew then that I was different from other people and that we weren't treated as equals.

"I was unhappy about it, but I recall that when I told my mother about the incident she passed it off with the comment that there were all kinds of people in the world and we just ignored people like that.

"That was one of very few exposures I had to prejudice while we were living in the South. Parents tended to warn their children repeatedly, from a very early age, 'Don't do this, and don't go there, and don't sass the man,' so they shielded them and insisted that they avoid situations where they would be mistreated. I don't recall any really unpleasant cases of discrimination in Arkansas because I avoided them."

In 1933 Johnson's family, having saved some money, moved to Chicago hoping to achieve a better life. John's parents were unable to find steady work, for the nation was in the midst of a depression and even many white people were unemployed. At one point they were forced to go on welfare for about a year.

"We were always poor when I was young, and always had all the characteristics of poor people," the publisher says. "I must confess I didn't suffer any special feeling of inferiority because of it. I always had the feeling that my mother was doing all that she could do, and, since most of the people that I knew intimately weren't doing any better than I was, I didn't have the feeling of being deprived. I knew I was poor, and I didn't like it, but I was always determined to move out of that category. Frankly, I never had any doubts that I would."

Johnson first attended Wendell Phillips High School in Chicago, but when that school burned down he was transferred to the new DuSable High School, which was named after the first settler in Chicago, a black named Jean Baptiste Pointe DuSable. Johnson was in the first class to graduate from the school in 1936.

To supplement his mother's income, Johnson worked while in high school for the National Youth Administration. He also found time to serve as editor of the school newspaper, to be president of his class and of the student body, and to study hard enough to graduate with honors. These activities gave him a feeling of identity and importance for the first time in his life, and as a consequence he enjoyed school. He credits a white teacher, Miss Mary Herrick, with having a strong motivational influence on him during his high school years.

It was John's superior performance in high school that enabled him to meet Harry H. Pace, the president of Supreme Life Insurance Company, which was then and still is the largest black business in the North. The meeting occurred when he was honored at an Urban League luncheon along with many other black students who had finished high school with honors.

"Mr. Pace was the main speaker at this affair, and I was introduced along with the other students. After the meeting was over I went up to shake his hand and tell him how much I enjoyed his talk. He asked me what my plans were and I told him I wanted very much to go to college, but that I didn't have enough money to go. He asked me how would I like to work part time at Supreme and go to college part time and, naturally, I thought it was a good idea so I agreed."

Johnson reported for work at Supreme's offices on September 1, 1936. He attended the University of Chicago in the morning, and worked as "assistant and handyman" on *The Supreme Liberty Guardian*, the firm's house magazine, in the afternoon. Initially, his chores included taking copy to the printer, reading proof, and handling engravings. Eventually, after he had gained experience, he was made editor of the publication, and he finally dropped out of college to give it his full time.

Johnson was then 18. Today, at 51, he is chairman of the insurance company's board, and its largest single stockholder.

Johnson's experience at Supreme was valuable in many ways. In addition to the experience he gained as editor of the magazine, he was exposed to many of the prominent black businessmen on Chicago's south side, where the firm was headquartered. "I think working at the insurance company and seeing for the first time that black men could manage businesses successfully gave me the feeling that I could do it, too," Johnson says.

In order to gather material for Supreme's magazine, Johnson prepared a monthly digest of news about blacks that appeared in national publications. This effort inspired the notion of producing a monthly publication featuring articles about successful blacks, and he discussed the idea with his employer. Pace encouraged him, but was unwilling to lend financial support unless it was unavailable from any other source.

Johnson composed a letter offering charter subscriptions in his new publication, *Negro Digest,* and mailed out twenty thousand copies of the letter after mortgaging his mother's furniture for five hundred dollars to cover the cost. Three thousand people subscribed to the publication and at a rate of two dollars each, Johnson had six thousand dollars to get the magazine off the ground.

Five thousand copies of the first issue were printed in November, 1942. Johnson dealt with Supreme's printer and obtained credit for the first printing, probably because the printer thought the project was being launched by the insurance company. When the enterprising youngster had difficulty getting a magazine distributor to place the publication on newsstands, he had friends call on news dealers asking for the publication until the demand for the magazine appeared so high that the distributor decided to handle it. Then he bought up the copies himself so the publication would appear to be a smashing success.

The circulation of *Negro Digest* grew rapidly, and in 1945, his venture a success, Johnson launched *Ebony*, which put heavy emphasis on photographs, in the style of *Life* magazine. Unlike *Negro Digest, Ebony* accepted advertising, but initially its publisher experienced little success in securing ads from major firms.

The problem, Johnson decided, was the fact that the lower echelon employees with whom he was dealing did not dare risk advertising in *Ebony* because they did not know how the major executives of their company would react. The publisher decided that, if he was to win any major accounts, it would be necessary for him to get approval from the top of the corporate hierarchy.

Johnson began writing letters to the heads of companies, telling them he wanted to discuss their policy toward the market that existed in the black community, but he got little response. When he began making personal calls, most secretaries would not give him appointments with their bosses.

"I finally began pointing out to them that if the president of the smallest nation in the world came to the United States he would be able to see the President as a matter of public policy and protocol," Johnson says. "I appealed to them on the basis that even though I was president of a very small company their president should have a moral obligation—one president to another—to see me."

The strategy worked. Johnson's first major corporate client was Zenith Radio Corporation, which has advertised in *Ebony* ever since. Other firms soon fell in line, and the success of the new publication was assured. Today, a million people subscribe to *Ebony*, and another two hundred thousand copies are sold on newsstands. *Jet*, a weekly newsmagazine, sells about five hundred thousand copies a week, and *Tan,* a magazine for women, has a circulation of two hundred thousand a month.

When it became apparent that his venture was a financial success, Johnson began searching for quarters in which to house the growing enterprise. He spotted a mortuary on the edge of the ghetto on South Michigan Avenue which appeared to offer promise as a home for the editorial and business offices of the magazines, but it took all of his wit and cunning to buy it.

The white man who owned the mortuary, although he was leaving the neighborhood because it was in the process of racial change, still was unwilling to sell his building to a black man. He turned down Johnson's offer of sixty thousand dollars for the property.

Johnson engaged a white attorney to negotiate for the property without revealing that he was the prospective buyer. He had never seen the inside of the building, so the attorney called the owner and told him that he wanted to have his maintenance man inspect the building before he made an offer on it. Johnson donned overalls, and went to the property and made a leisurely inspection. He liked what he saw, and the white lawyer finally bought the place for $52,000—eight thousand dollars less than Johnson had originally been willing to pay! The structure is no longer adequate for the thriving enterprise, and a new headquarters is being built near Chicago's Loop.

Johnson's original publication, *Negro Digest,* was discontinued in 1951 because it was losing money, but he began publishing it again in 1961, as a vehicle for articles by rising young black authors. The magazine still loses between eighty and one hundred thousand dollars a year, but Johnson continues it out of a sense of responsibility toward young black literary talents.

Johnson says he believes the most significant contribution of his magazines to be the early attention they gave to black history. In the late 1950's *Ebony* commissioned Lerone

Bennett to do a series of articles on black history which ran in the magazine in 1960. Ultimately, they were compiled into a book, *Before the Mayflower*. This effort, the publisher feels, gave the magazine's readers a sense of identity—a sense of their heritage—which was an important contribution to black progress.

"I also feel that, by seeking out black people who are engaged in business and by recording and photographing and mirroring their achievements so that other people can see them and be inspired by them, we have also made a contribution," the publisher says.

"Whenever a new voice has come on the horizon, *Ebony* has not been afraid to tackle the story. For example, we were the first major national publication to do a story on Stokely Carmichael at a time when many other people were shying away from him. We recently did a story on the black revolution, and we had a long story by Huey P. Newton, who is the organizer of the Black Panthers.

"I think when there are new voices in the black community a publisher has an obligation to expose those views to the readers and to the people involved. I think we have done that, but more than anything else I think we have furnished information to black people so that they can be proud of their heritage.

"We have inspired young people to move to a greater achievement by knowing what other people have achieved. I also think we have sort of been a channel of communications between blacks and whites. The whites can read the magazine (5 percent of the circulation is white) and know what blacks are doing, and we run just enough stories about whites so that blacks can read and know what many of the whites are doing."

After the success of his publishing business was assured, Johnson began venturing into other fields. In 1955, at the suggestion of Earl B. Dickerson, who was then president of Supreme Life Insurance Company, Johnson bought one thousand shares of stock in the company. Subsequently, with Dickerson's support, he won a place on Supreme's board of directors. He began acquiring additional stock, and in 1964 became Supreme's largest single stockholder. Today, he exercises a strong influence on the policies of the company in which he started as an office boy nearly thirty-five years ago.

Johnson, a nervously energetic man who neither drinks nor smokes and never takes vacations, lived until 1969 with his wife, Eunice, and their two children in an apartment in Hyde Park, an integrated neighborhood that surrounds the campus of the University of Chicago. They then purchased a condominium apartment in an exclusive building on North Lake Shore Drive. His mother, who is still very active, works occasionally in the community relations department of Johnson Publishing Company, handling the charitable activities of the firm. She also serves as its treasurer and vice-president.

"I tell my children that in the end their future success will depend on their own personal success and achievement," Johnson says. "I don't think it will depend on me, and it won't depend on their mother. It will depend on them as individuals. Just as the grades they get in school depend on the amount of homework and application they give to their studies, their achievement in life will really depend on how much they put into whatever they decide to do.

"I don't think parents ought to try to influence children to follow a particular line of work unless they want to do it. I hope that my son will want to enter the publishing business, but I won't feel badly if he doesn't.

"I simply tell my children that they should be responsible, that they should respect the rights of others, and that they should insist on being individuals free to do what they want to do as long as it doesn't interfere with the rights of others.

"I tell them that the opportunities they have will be dependent on the kind of training that they get, the kind of education that they have, and the kind of effort they are willing to put into what they do."

Thinking back on his own life, Johnson says that it is apparent that the effort he put into his own high school work, which won honors for him and enabled him to meet Mr. Pace, was the deciding factor in his career.

"If I hadn't worked hard in high school, I wouldn't have been honored, and I wouldn't have met Mr. Pace. Therefore, I would not have gone to work for the insurance company. I think there was a very good chance that I never would have been in business for myself. If I hadn't been able to do any one of those things I wouldn't be where I am today."

Johnson says he believes the most important thing for young blacks today is to believe in themselves—to believe in the existence of opportunities that haven't been there in years gone by, and the possibility of capitalizing on those opportunities.

"I know we are living in a sort of cynical age," Johnson says. "Young people tend to discount hope and belief and faith as being unrealistic and not relevant to life today. But I think we have to have hope, we have to have faith, we have to believe in people and believe in things. Most of all we have to believe in ourselves.

"I always had the feeling that I was going to make it. I might have ended up disillusioned and disappointed, but fortunately I was able to achieve some measure of success. But I always thought I would. I never thought I wouldn't. I always worked with that in mind.

"I didn't know when I would achieve or how I would achieve it, but I believed that I would. I think much of that goes back to my mother, who was a very strong personality and who had a great belief in the future. She constantly pounded into me that I could do anything I really wanted to do.

"I think there is a tendency now for young people to assume that anything old is bad, that everything that has been here before they came should be removed and abolished. I think that is the wrong attitude. I think their attitude should be to build on what they see and what is here now. This does not mean that you have to follow in the path of your father, but that you can go beyond what he did; you can blaze a new path; you can do all of that without trying to destroy what he has done.

"I also feel that as young people grow older they will realize that their elders, in most instances, did the best they could under the circumstances in which they lived."

Johnson says that blacks can achieve a great deal by group activity, particularly in winning public offices and putting pressure on government to seek solutions to social problems. In the end, however, he says, "real achievement must be a one person thing."

"Every black is obligated to do all that he can to achieve for himself," the publisher says. "If he makes something of himself he also contributes favorably to the total image of black people.

"I recall Dean William Hastie writing that black people should make the most of all the opportunities they have, while striving to improve those opportunities. That means that even if a youngster must attend an inferior segregated school he should attend it, and get the most he can from it, while fighting hard to have it improved to the level of other schools in the community.

"The ability of blacks to win a full share of America no longer depends primarily on our ability to demand new opportunities to participate. It depends on how well our youngsters prepare themselves to cope with the opportunities that already exist."

14

James Farmer

Poor Man's Friend in Washington

James Farmer's earliest recollection of his childhood, when he was a little boy in Holly Springs, Mississippi, is of a bitter taste of the racial discrimination which ultimately led him to become an activist for civil rights.

"I went shopping in downtown Holly Springs with my mother," Farmer recalls, "and as we were walking back home I was thirsty so I told her that I would like to get a Coke. She told me that I couldn't get one there, and would have to wait until we got home.

"Just then we were passing a drug store and I looked in the door and saw another little boy having a Coke at the soda fountain, so I said to my mother, 'He's having a Coke. I want one, too.'

"'You can't have one,' she repeated.

"I was really thirsty, and I wasn't to be put off. I said again, 'He's having one. Why can't I?' and I continued to press her until she was finally forced to say what she had hoped to avoid.

"'Well,' she said, not looking at me, 'it's because you are colored and he is white.'

"I didn't understand it then, but I sensed that I should say no more, and we walked in silence the rest of the way home."

189

Farmer says it was no accident that some fifteen years later, when he became the founding father of the Congress of Racial Equality, CORE's first active programs were aimed at discrimination against blacks in places of public accommodation. He was still haunted by that first childhood revelation of second class citizenship, and had "reacted angrily" to all the similar indignities that he endured in the years that followed. They became for him "a major preoccupation," and he vowed that he would not rest until black people were fully accepted in all of the places where "white folks" could go.

"In later years," Farmer says, "I began to see that the greater urgency and highest priority revolved around the need for jobs and other social and economic problems. But in those early days what irritated the black middle class was not being able to eat dinner in the restaurant of your choice, and not being able to sit down and have a Coke wherever you chose."

Today, Farmer is very much concerned with the larger needs. As one of the highest ranking blacks in the Nixon administration he is directly involved in the solution of most of the nation's most pressing social problems.

Farmer says he took the post as Assistant Secretary of Health, Education, and Welfare because "there is a great need for black people to get on the inside and try to have some influence. It is important that we not just stand outside and criticize. A black American is still an American."

"I accepted the job because I think there is a great opportunity, if given considerable leeway, to get some things done that are important to black Americans and to all Americans. HEW is where the action is, where the action should be, and where I think the action will be," he says.

Farmer does not believe that in the past the nation has gotten the mileage it should from the fifty billion dollars a year that is spent by his department. The poor people are still poor, and welfare has tended to mire people into reliance on the dole, rather than helping them to survive until they become productive citizens. He believes that a guaranteed income or negative income tax of some sort is the answer.

"The welfare system is arbitrary and demeaning in regulations and practice," Farmer says. "The man in the house provision, for example, forces fathers to leave home so that their kids can eat. We now understand that in spite of the welfare system there is hunger and starvation—children with brain damage beyond control by the time they are four years old. The argument that a guaranteed income would destroy incentive is hogwash. All of us are on welfare, being subsidized by the government, one way or another. Industry, farmers receive millions in subsidy, but it hasn't destroyed their initiative, or incentive, or motivation. Let's make it equitable."

Secretary Farmer is equally critical of health and educational programs. He says he was urged to join HEW to devise new programs, improve delivery systems, tighten up the organizational structure, evaluate, change, and innovate. If he does it with the vigor that led him to a position of national leadership in the civil rights movement at the age of twenty-one, there is hope that new solutions may be found to some of the problems that plague America.

Farmer was born in Marshall, Texas, on January 12, 1920. His father was a teacher at Wiley College, with a stable source of income, so the family was not poor in the sense that most blacks in the South were poor. However, the elder Farmer's salary was meager, and far below that of white teachers of similar educational attainment and intellectual capacity.

During Farmer's early childhood, although his father had earned a Ph.D., his income was only one hundred and fifty dollars a month. When he was offered three hundred dollars a month by the Gammon Theological Seminary in Atlanta in 1930 it seemed to the family a sum too fabulous to imagine.

Jim Farmer's paternal grandparents were both born slaves in South Carolina and neither of them had any education whatsoever. Their son, despite his impoverished family circumstances, finished elementary school in Georgia, where the family then lived. He wanted to continue his education, but there was no high school for blacks in the entire state of Georgia. Undaunted, he sought admission to Bethune-Cookman Institute and walked from Georgia to Daytona Beach, Florida, to enroll in the school.

He finished at Bethune-Cookman with a straight A average, and then walked and hitchhiked from Daytona Beach to Boston where he applied and was accepted for admission to Boston University. While attending college, he worked full-time as a carriage boy for a wealthy white woman in order to support himself and send money back home to support his parents. His father had gone blind and could no longer work. He was graduated from Boston University magna cum laude.

After graduation, Farmer's father immediately began working on his Ph.D. There were some courses he couldn't get at Boston University so he enrolled at Harvard where he again completed all of his courses with a grade of A. He finished all of his work for the Ph.D., including the dissertation, in a single year! Unfortunately, the university required that Ph.D. candidates be in residence for two years, so he had to remain in Boston for another year in order to fulfill that requirement and get his degree.

A minister as well as a teacher, Dr. Farmer was a remarkable scholar who spoke and wrote fluently in Hebrew, Greek, Aramaic, Latin, French, German, and several other languages.

"I admired, almost stood in awe of him," his son says. "He never went to a movie. If he wanted to relax he'd grab a book in Hebrew, in which he had taken his doctorate, take the dog for a walk in the country, and sit under a tree and read the book.

"Father and his library—five or six thousand books—motivated me a great deal. He made me use it. When I asked him a question he rarely gave me the answer. He would suggest several places where I might find it, and then the next day would ask me the same question to see if I had looked it up and found the answer. I will always be totally grateful that he insisted that I read."

Farmer attended elementary school in a number of southern communities in which his father taught. His sister and brother were younger than he. They played school together. By the time he started school he already knew how to read.

"When I entered first grade I was considerably ahead of the other kids and I was quickly pushed up from 1A to 1B," Farmer recalls. "The next year I was pushed up another half grade in an effort to get me among students at whose level I would be. In total, I skipped two grades, and when I entered Wiley College at the age of fourteen I was still a kid who should have been playing stickball in short pants. The other students were seventeen and eighteen, which is quite an age gap when you are in your teens. A girl of seventeen is a woman. A fourteen-year-old boy is a child. This worked a social handicap on me that it took a long time to overcome."

Farmer won a four-year scholarship to Wiley College amounting to $250 a year, and in 1934, living at home, it was ample to pay for his education. He was an accomplished public speaker, and got the scholarship as an award for winning a high school oratorical contest. He also debated during his senior year in high school, and during his freshman year at Wiley, and for the remaining three years was captain of Wiley's debate team. It was an experience that proved of enormous value when he assumed a leadership role in the civil rights movement in later years.

The young student majored in chemistry and biology, intending to become a physician, but he changed his mind about that in his senior year. He played tennis and boxed, and says he had a good punch and good ring generalship, but didn't like to get hit. That reluctance seems dubious, for the six-foot, 210-pound civil rights activist certainly displayed no physical timidity during protest demonstrations and "freedom rides" in the years that followed.

Farmer says that his academic record in college was not what it should have been (some B-pluses were sprinkled among the A's) because he found that he could make good grades without studying. He once complained to his father that he was doing A work in his course and couldn't understand why Dad was giving him B's. Dr. Farmer told his son sternly that he was disappointed in him because he wasn't pushing himself, and for the remainder of the term gave him seven or eight books to read each week and then quizzed him on their contents. If the boy hadn't read them his father gave him "a long harangue" about the folly of wasting himself.

Farmer got his bachelor of science degree at Wiley in 1938, and the family then moved to Washington, D.C., where his father had taken a position at Howard University, teaching the New Testament and Greek. During his senior year Jim renounced his ambition to become a physician and decided to become a minister instead. He completed his studies at Howard in 1941 and received his bachelor of divinity degree, but then refused to be ordained.

"The occasion of that refusal was the announcement of the unification plan of the Methodist church—the Methodist Episcopal Church North and the Methodist Episcopal Church South," Farmer asserts. "They drew up a plan which was a segregated plan. It had six jurisdictions, five geographical and one—the central jurisdiction—which was racial. That jurisdiction included all of the black churches from Weehawken, Maine, to Chitlin' Switch, Georgia. That was more than I could stomach, so I refused to be ordained."

Instead of entering the ministry, Farmer began working for the Fellowship of Reconciliation, a pacifist organization, as race relations director. The following year he and a group of University of Chicago students organized CORE as a pilot project to experiment with the use of the techniques of nonviolent protest and passive resistance that Mohandas K. Ghandi had practiced in India. During the following year another dozen chapters were organized in other cities, and at twenty-two Farmer became the first chairman of the national organization.

In June of 1943 CORE conducted the first successful sit-in demonstration at a restaurant in the Chicago Loop, and subsequently created another protest device called the "standing line," persistently waiting in line in places where blacks were being denied admission.

In that same year Farmer moved to New York and for several years worked as an organizer for various movements, finally becoming national program director for the NAACP. Throughout this period, however, he retained his relationship with CORE as chairman of the National Action Committee. From 1943 to 1961 CORE continued to grow and began to raise a budget for its activities. Its techniques became increasingly popular, and in 1961 Farmer resigned from NAACP to devote all of his time to CORE. He remained in his new post as national director until 1966.

Throughout this period Farmer participated in or led countless protest activities. He was jailed for his efforts for forty days in 1961. In 1963 he was jailed for leading a civil rights demonstration in Plaquemine, Louisiana. That was the year that CORE launched another innovation in protest—the Freedom Ride—which soon found its way into the vocabulary. Groups of riders went South to determine the extent to which bus terminals had been desegregated as the federal law required. They were physically attacked in Alabama and arrested in Mississippi, but the tactic finally forced compliance throughout the South with the 1960 U.S. Supreme Court decision.

On August 28, 1963, Farmer spoke, along with A. Philip Randolph, Roy Wilkins, and the late Dr. Martin Luther King, during the March on Washington, the largest single protest demonstration in the history of the United States. More than two hundred thousand protesters were on hand to hear Dr. King give his most enduring speech, "I have a dream . . ."

Between June 10 and 16, 1965, Farmer participated in mass demonstrations and marches to the Chicago City Hall to protest the slow pace of desegregation of the city's school system. He was again arrested, along with comedian Dick Gregory and 224 others.

Farmer left CORE in 1966 to launch the Center for Community Action Education, which was to wage a national campaign against functional illiteracy. He thought he had a commitment of financial support from the federal government, but after he had left CORE the Office of Economic Opportunity refused to fund the project.

Disappointed at this rebuff after he had acted in good faith, Farmer turned to teaching. He accepted a professorship at Lincoln University in Pennsylvania during 1966 and 1967, and the following year lectured a few days a month at Lincoln, also serving as a professor of adult education at New York University. During this period he also lectured at more than one hundred colleges and universities a year, until he was appointed to his present post as Assistant Secretary of Health, Education, and Welfare for Administration in February, 1969.

In his present responsibility Farmer is concerned with

the social needs of Americans of all races, creeds, and nationalities. He decries the hostilities and lack of understanding that divide deprived citizens of different racial and ethnic origins.

"You hear some white people only one generation removed from absolute poverty and still on the bottom rung of the economic ladder who argue that their parents or grandparents came to this country poor and uneducated and worked their way out of poverty, and that black Americans should do likewise.

"They forget that when their parents and grandparents came to America, although they were poor and living in the slums and the ghettos, they were also virtually indistinguishable from the people who lived outside," Farmer says. "They were white. All they had to do was put on a new suit and learn the language and they could walk right across the line. It is not that easy for the black man. It doesn't even help him to change his name.

"Black people are the only group in the history of this country that have been victimized by the racist theory that they are, by nature, by Act of God, inferior, and that those whose skins are white are superior. Those who came from Europe may have been disliked, but they were not considered an inferior breed.

"Finally, none of the other groups had been slaves here in this country. The black man is in the historically unique position of being the descendant of former slaves and is seeking a rapprochement with the descendants of those who owned his ancestors."

Farmer says he sees black Americans as becoming "proud and equal partners" in a pluralistic culture. In his view, America is not a melting pot, and he says he has stopped referring to it as a melting pot because it has not melted anything. It has not democratized people. Most people, even though their families have been in the country for generations, continue to maintain an ethnic identity of which they are proud, yet they are also integrated into the framework of the nation.

"The black man, on the contrary, has tried to avoid developing any identity," Farmer says. "He has rejected an identity. He has sought to become white and lose any identification with a group, to forget that he is a member of a group, to get a little money and a little education, be culturally assimilated as an individual, and become a white person with an invisible black skin.

"This just isn't going to work, so I think we must come to the realization that the nation is not a melting pot but a pluralistic society and that people do not enter a pluralistic society as individuals, they enter as a group or fail to enter as a group. They enter as a cultural entity, and then, once they have entered—as an ethnic group or as a cultural group—individuals within that group make it or fail to make it as individuals."

Farmer sees the black power movement, and the achievement of ethnic cohesiveness of the black community, as the short-term goal of blacks. Once that cohesiveness has been achieved and black people know who they are, have pride in their identity, and have achieved greater political and economic power as a group, they can take their place in a pluralistic society among other people who retain an ethnic identity and succeed individually on their own merits.

"Black power is reprogramming ourselves," he says, "brainwashing ourselves, and it has also pointed up certain programmatic thrusts that are needed: the need for community control of institutions, the need for the economic development of the black community. It has also revealed the need for more effective political organization and political action in the black community to use our vote as a weapon to reward our friends and punish our enemies."

The achievement of black power requires militance on

the part of black people, Farmer says, but militance is not synonymous with violence. It is simply "an unwillingness to compromise on matters of principle," and consequently is not negative, but positive.

As one who was militant himself at an early age, Secretary Farmer has little difficulty understanding the motives of most of the militant students on the college campuses today. He believes that they are demonstrating to find answers to a very real question: How can the underrepresented poor, black, and young Americans be brought into the decision-making processes of society.

"I don't always agree with the tactics that they use," he says. "Wherever there is violence or destruction of property it should be considered wrong and unacceptable. Anyone who violates the law must accept arrest as a consequence, and I speak from experience.

"But I do have sympathy with the college groups that make nonnegotiable demands upon university and college administrations. I am an old trade union organizer and know that the way you negotiate is to go in with excessive demands. Guns and violence or potential violence are wrong, but demands are not wrong. Even when they say the demands are nonnegotiable, that is not unusual, either. I did it as a trade union organizer."

Farmer believes that there are many more opportunities today for middle-class blacks, for those who have skills, and those who have education. But he says that they are not significantly better for the unskilled, who have become increasingly obsolete as machines have taken over the jobs that they once won.

"That's why education is so terribly important, and why it must be improved," he says. "One of the great tragedies is that the disruptive youngsters in our schools tend to be the brightest and the most imaginative, but when they see the irrelevance of what they are learning and the stupidity of the kind of teaching that many of them go through, they are not prepared to take it. They are misguided when they drop out, for any education is better than none, but I think the fault lies with the schools and not with the kids.

"I think that the fault also often lies with the parents, and we are going to have to work on them while we are working on the schools and the children. Perhaps we even need to work on the parents to a greater extent than the children. We have to develop among our people, parents and children alike, a love of learning and a yearning for excellence.

"We have seen this among some other groups and it has served them well, but we blacks have not had it. We have seen it among Jews, for example, and it has certainly served them well."

Farmer plans, in his role as a major executive in the second largest federal agency, to spend a great deal of time developing programs to deal with early childhood development. He wants to create an office of childhood development to work on the needs of children in their first five years. He also hopes to develop a prenatal program for parents in which they will be taught the awesome responsibility of bringing children into the world and bringing them up. Parents will be taught about the need to stimulate the child's curiosity and creativity, to develop in him a hunger for learning and knowledge, and to make play a learning experience. Farmer would like to lend educational toys to the poor for their children to use.

"I think we are going to have to work on all aspects of the environment that affect our children," Farmer says. "It is the only way we can make significant changes in their outlook on life and stimulate the advancement of black people in this country. That's where I think we can make a real input at HEW."

"I feel about all black children as I feel about my own," Secretary Farmer concludes. "I want for them a better life.

I want for them what they want for themselves. I want them not even to have to deal with the problems of racism because the problems will have been dealt with by the time they are adults.

"What black people really want and need is not really very complex, nor is it an unreasonable demand. The most important thing for us is to be accepted as human beings. If we can have that much from this society we'll make it the rest of the way by ourselves."

Index

INDEX

INDEX

Guevara, Che, 42
*Guide to Negro History in America,
A* (Drotning), ix

Hamilton, West, 110
Hampton, Lionel, 31
Harvard University, 192
Hastie, Dean William, 188
Hatcher, Richard, 85-101
  childhood, 87-90
  education, 91-93
  family, 87-92
  as mayor, 96, 97
  mayoral campaign, 94-97
  viewpoint, 98-101
Hatcher family, 87
Hearn, Ethel, 172
Hellum, Mr., 25
Henley, William Ernest, 144
Herrick, Mary, 181
Highland Park High School, 61
Ho Chi Minh, 42
Horn and Hardart Company, 138
House Agriculture committee, 133
Howard University, 104, 107, 108,
  110, 112, 194
Howard University Medical School,
  104, 111
Howland School, 163
Hughes, Langston, 172, 173
Hyde Park High School, 51

Illinois Central Railroad, 126
Indiana University, 86, 93
Invictus (Henley), 144
Iowa Central College, 162

Jackson, Jesse, 19-43, 156
  as athlete, 29-31
  childhood, 19, 22, 23-26
  education of, 27, 28
  family, 23, 24, 28, 29
  as minister, 20, 21, 34, 35
  on religion, 32, 33
Jackson, Mrs. Jesse, 33
Jackson, Jesse, Jr., 33
Jackson, Jonathan Luther, 33
Jackson, Santita, 33
James Brown Enterprises, 81
James Brown Productions, 81
James Brown Show, 81
Jefferson, Thomas, x
Jet, 177, 183

Jobs program, 153
Joe Louis Milk Company, 36, 37
John Marshall College, 52
John Marshall Law School, 53
Johnson, James Weldon, 172 173
Johnson, John H., 177-188
  childhood, 179, 180
  education, 180, 181
  family, 179, 186
  viewpoint, 177-179, 186-188
Johnson, Mrs. John H., 186
Johnson, Lyndon B., 153
Johnson Publishing Company, 186
Jones, LeRoi, 41
Juliet Lowe Upper Grade Center,
  164

Kansas City Monarchs, 8, 9
Karenga, Ron, 41
Kenyatta, Jomo, 42
Kerner report, 130
King, Martin Luther, Jr., 20, 27, 33,
  41-43, 44, 54, 82, 174, 196
  assassination of, 22

Langford, Anna Riggs, 44-57
  childhood, 44-47
  education, 48-52
  family, 45-47, 49
  as lawyer, 53, 54
  viewpoint, 55-57
Langford, Larry, Jr., 53, 56
Langford, Lawrence C., 53
Lee, John C. H., 66
Lee, Robert E., 66
Legal Aid Society, 53
L'Enfant, Pierre, x
Life, 177, 183
Lincoln University, 63, 64, 196
Lindsay, John, 139, 140
Locke, Alain, 108
Lombardi, Vince, 12
London *Times*, 95
Look, 177
Louis, Joe, 26
Luce, Henry, 177
Lumumba, Patrice, 42

Malcolm X, 41
Marshall, Thurgood, 52
Massachusetts Institute of Technol-
  ogy, 66

205

INDEX

McKinley Music Company, 170
McKissick, Floyd, 33
Meharry Medical College, 105
Militancy, 13, 56, 69, 70, 72, 99-100, 156, 167, 174, 178, 198, 199
Montgomery movement, 27

National Action Committee, 195
National Association for the Advancement of Colored People, 52, 104, 111, 195
National Baseball League, 2, 10
Eastern Division, 17, 18
Most Valuable Player award, 10
National Honor Society, 107
National Youth Administration, 181
Negro Digest, 175, 177, 182-184
Negro Vanguard, The (Bardolph), xi
Newton, Heuy P., 185
New York City Department of Hospital Services, 138
New York Life Insurance Company, 151
New York Mets, 17, 18
New York State Assembly, 138
New York Times, 95
New York University, 196
Nkrumah, Kwame, 42
North Carolina Agricultural and Technical Institute, 31, 33, 42
North Carolina Intercollegiate Council on Human Rights, 31
Northeastern Illinois State College, 173

Office of Economic Opportunity, 196
199th Light Infantry Brigade, 102, 115
Open housing marches, 33, 44
Operation Breadbasket, 20, 21, 33, 34, 37, 38, 39
Opportunities Industrialization Centers, 34
"Our People" (TV show), 59

Pace, Harry H., 181, 182, 187
Parent-Teacher Association, 158
Pennsylvania Railroad, 126
Pennsylvania State University, 108
Pentagon, the, 112, 114, 115
Poverty, 23, 39, 40

Procaccino, Mario, 139
Proctor, Sam, 32
Protest demonstrations, 31, 33, 39, 44, 86, 195, 196
Protest marches, 33, 44
Pulitzer Prize, 170, 173
Pullman Standard Company, 87, 93

Racial discrimination, 13, 22, 25, 26, 31, 44, 45, 49, 50, 57, 62-65, 85, 86, 123-125, 136, 137, 145, 146, 169, 172, 179, 180, 189, 190
in education, 27, 30
in U.S. Army, 104, 105, 113, 114, 116, 117
Randolph, A. Philip, 196
Reader's Digest, 177
Religion, 20, 21, 23, 24, 32-36, 77, 90, 147, 161, 194, 195
Reserve Officers Training Corps, 64, 110-112
Riggs, Grandfather, 45
Riggs, Mrs. (mother of Anna Langford), 45
Riggs, James, 51
Riggs family, 50
Riots, 82, 174
in Chicago, 54
in Watts, 130
"Riots" (Brooks), 174
Robinson, Jackie, 4
Robinson, Leonard, 42, 43
Rock Island Railroad, 112, 120, 126, 127
Roosevelt University, 52
Rush, Bobby, 72

Sandburg, Carl, 175
San Francisco Giants, 30
Scandinavian Airlines Systems, Inc., 74
Seaway National Bank, 3
Shattuck, Mr., 121
Shepherd, Mr. (father of John Shepherd), 145
Shepherd, Mrs. (mother of John Shepherd), 148
Shepherd, Andrea, 152
Shepherd, Denise, 152
Shepherd, Frances, 147
Shepherd, John, 143-156

INDEX

childhood, 144-150
education, 151
family, 144-150, 152
viewpoint, 143, 144, 154-156
Shepherd, Mrs. John, 151, 152
Shepherd, Laurie, 152
Simmons, Curt, 9
Sit-ins, 31, 86, 195
Slavery, 105, 125
"Song In the Front Yard, A" (Brooks), 171
Southern Christian Leadership Conference, 21, 34
Southern Normal High School, 161
Sterling High School, 29
Street in Bronzeville, A (Brooks), 173
Student Advanced Infantry Officer Course, 112, 113
Sullivan, Leon, 34
Sumner-Magruder elementary school, 107
Sunflower Laundry, 146
Supreme Liberty Guardian, The, 181
Supreme Life Insurance Company, 177, 181, 182, 185, 186

T. R. Miller Mill Company, 157
Talladega College, 162
Tan, 177, 184
Tan Son Nhut air base, 82
Tet offensive, 102, 115
Third Training Brigade, 115
366th Infantry Regiment, 110
370th Armored Infantry Battalion, 112, 113
371st Infantry Regiment, 110
Tilmon, James, 58-74
childhood, 58, 61, 62
education, 63, 64
family, 61, 62
as pilot, 67, 68
in U.S. Army, 64-67
viewpoint, 69-74
Tilmon, Mrs. James, 61
Tilmon family, 61, 62
Truth, Sojourner, 151
Try Me Music, 81
Turner, Nat, 41

Universal Oil Products Company, 153

University of Chicago, 14, 181, 195
University of Illinois, 30, 105, 173
University of Wisconsin, 173
Urban League, 181
U.S. Air Force, 67
U.S. Army, 4, 64-67, 102, 103, 110-112, 151
racial discrimination in, 104, 105, 113, 114, 116, 117
U.S. Congress, 132, 133, 139
U.S. Constitution, 54
U.S. Department of Health, Education, and Welfare, 134, 190, 191, 200
U.S. Department of Labor, 134
U.S. House of Representatives, 132, 133
U.S. Steel Company, 93
U.S. Supreme Court, 52, 196

Valparaiso University, 93
Venetian Blind Company, 151
Veterans committee, 134
Veterans of Foreign Wars, 31
Vietnam War, 82, 102, 103, 115, 117

Wallace, DeWitt, 177
War College, 114
Washington, Booker T., 41, 43, 177, 178
Washington, George, 174
Watts, riots in, 130
Watts Savings and Loan Association, 130
Wendell Phillips High School, 180
Wescott, Charles, 89
White, Walter, 41, 175
"Why Fliers and Drivers Should Not Drink" (Langford), 48
Wiley College, 191, 193, 194
Wilkins, Roy, 41, 99, 175, 196
Williams, Paul R., 121
Wilson Junior College, 173
World Series, 17, 18
Wrigley Field, 3, 8, 10, 17
WTTW-TV, 59

Young, Whitney, 41
Young Men's Christian Association, 3, 5, 6, 7, 50

Zenith Radio Corporation, 183